D1219791

THINKERS OF OUR TIME

HEIDEGGER

THINKERS OF OUR TIME

HEIDEGGER

by

David E. Cooper

Everett Library
Queens College
1900 Selwyn Ave.
Charlotte, NC 28274

The Claridge Press
London

193
H362c

All rights reserved. No part of this publication may be reproduced or transmitted in any form or by any means, including photocopying and recording, without the written permission of the copyright holder, application for which should be addressed to the Publishers. Such written permission must also be obtained before any part of this publication is stored in a retrieval system of any nature.

First published in Great Britain 1996

by The Claridge Press
33 Canonbury Park South
London
N1 2JW

Copyright © David E. Cooper

Printed by
Antony Rowe Ltd
Chippenham

CIP data for this title is available from the British Library

ISBN 1-870626-12-5

Cooper, David E.: *Heidegger*

1.   Political Science
2.   Philosophy

CONTENTS

Abbreviations

BP *The Basic Problems of Phenomenology*. Tr. A. Hofstadter. Bloomington: Indiana University Press, 1982.

BQ *Basic Questions of Philosophy*. Tr. R. Rojcewicz & A. Schuwer. Bloomington: Indiana University Press, 1994.

BT *Being and Time*. Tr. J. Macquarrie & E. Robinson. Oxford: Blackwell, 1980.

BW *Basic Writings*. Ed. D.F. Krell. London: Routledge & Kegan Paul, 1978.

DT *Discourse on Thinking*. Tr. J. Anderson & E.H. Freund. New York: Harper & Row, 1966.

EB *Existence and Being*. Ed. W. Brock. Chicago: Regnery, 1949.

EG *Early Greek Thinking: the dawn of Western philosophy*. Tr. D.F. Krell & F. Capuzzi. San Francisco: Harper & Row, 1984.

GA *Gesamtausgabe*. Frankfurt: Klostermann, 1975- . (References to the Collected Works are to Volume number and page number).

HC *The Heidegger Controversy: a critical reader*. Ed. R. Wolin. Cambridge, Mass.: MIT Press, 1993 (Contains various pieces by and on Heidegger, relating to his Nazi involvement).

HCT *History of the Concept of Time: Prologomena*. Tr. T. Kiesel. Bloomington: Indiana University Press, 1985.

ID *Identity and Difference.* Tr. J. Stambaugh. New York: Harper & Row, 1969.

IM *An Introduction to Metaphysics.* Tr. R. Mannheim. New Haven: Yale University Press, 1959.

N *Nietzsche: Band II.* Pfullingen: Neske, 1961.

Ne *Nietzsche Vol.4: Nihilism.* Tr. F. Capuzzi. San Francisco: Harper & Row, 1982.

PLT *Poetry, Language, Thought.* Tr. A. Hofstadter. New York: Harper & Row, 1975.

QCT *The Question Concerning Technology (and other essays).* Tr. W. Lovitt. New York: Harper & Row, 1977.

R 'The Rectorate 1933/34: Facts and Thoughts'. Tr. K. Harries. *Review of Metaphysics*, **38**, 1985.

TB *On Time and Being.* Tr. J. Stambaugh. New York: Harper

1. Introduction

'One of the greatest philosophers of the twentieth century'; 'one of the two greatest philosophers of our century'; 'incontestably the greatest thinker of the age'. Here, in ascending dithyrambic order, are three estimates of the German philosopher Martin Heidegger culled from the hundreds of books devoted to his work over the last few years. Only the other philosopher intended in the second eulogy, Ludwig Wittgenstein, can compete for such plaudits, but not even he rivals Heidegger in influence beyond the confines of philosophy: upon theology, literary criticism and environmental thought, and even, so I'm told, nursing studies. For the poet Paul Celan and the theologian Rudolf Bultmann, as much as for any philosopher, Heidegger has been 'The Thinker' of our century.

There is another respect in which the cases of Heidegger and Wittgenstein differ. Even those who are far from being 'Wittgensteinians' concede the Austrian's genius and regard his views as serious, worthy competitors to their own. Heidegger, on the other hand, was the favourite whipping-boy during the 1930s and '40s of the Logical Positivists, who enjoyed citing such utterances as 'The Nothing nothings itself' as paradigms of the worst metaphysical nonsense. For post-war Oxford philosophy, as one of its luminaries recalls, Heidegger was a 'joke' and students were protected from exposure to him. Even today, in departments oriented towards 'analytic' philosophy, Heidegger often puts in only a fleeting appearance, perhaps as a dark precursor to Sartre on an Existentialism course that suffices for coverage of 'continental' philosophy.

The 'reek of incense' wafting from Heideggerian 'Perpetual Adoration Societies', which critical admirers of the philosopher have scented, continues to contend, then, with cold and hostile blasts. Hostility, like homage, does not come from philosophers alone. Günter Grass was not only parodying Heidegger's prose but bemoaning the man's influence on his father's generation when, in *Dog Years*, he has German officers in the last days of the war sending such communiqués as 'The Nothing is coming-to-be between enemy armour and our own spearheads... The Nothing will be after-accomplished on the double'. In *Old Masters*, the Austrian novelist Thomas Bernhard expressed his distaste more directly: 'Heidegger was always merely comical... a feeble thinker from the Alpine foothills... a ceaselessly gravid German philosophical cow... a tasteless pudding for the mediocre German mind'.

The intensity of such diatribes betrays, of course, an appreciation of the spell exerted by Heidegger on so many intellectuals over the last seventy years. Acolytes and critics alike might concur in — whilst differently interpreting — Iris Murdoch's enigmatic judgement that Heidegger was 'possibly Lucifer in person'. For a wider public, doubtless, Heidegger is of interest primarily because of the 'Heidegger affair' — the issue of his involvement with the Nazis during the 1930s. That affair began shortly after the war and was conducted in the pages of Sartre's journal, *Les Temps modernes*, with friends and foes disputing the degree and significance of that involvement. An on-and-off affair, it resumed with particular intensity after the publication of

Victor Farias' *Heidegger et le nazisme* in 1987, a book which, for all its inaccuracy and animosity, finally established the depth, if not the import, of Heidegger's involvement. Interest in the Heidegger affair, however, presupposes a fascination with his wider thought. Why, otherwise, should the sins of just this one German professor be singled out for attention? Why otherwise — except to those with merely biographical concerns — should the significance of Heidegger's involvement matter?

The reason for the influence and fascination exerted by Heidegger is surely this: the remarkable blend, in his writings, of abstract philosophical speculation with a critique of the modern human condition, of our 'destitute age' from which 'the Gods have fled'. The word 'blend' should be emphasized here, for while there have been many figures in the twentieth century who have been both speculative philosophers and critics of our times — Bertrand Russell, for example — the impression in their cases has been that of two disjoint activities being pursued. Where, one wonders, was the connection between Russell's theory of classes and his plea for sexual liberation? In the case of Heidegger, on the other hand, philosophy and critique are seamlessly inter-woven. The 'forgetfulness of Being' — his abiding theme — is at once held to be the crucial error of nearly all previous philoso-phers and the root of 'the darkening of the world', now become almost pitch-black in this, our age of 'dreary technological frenzy' (IM 37). Only in the writings of Nietzsche, perhaps, does one encounter a similar equation between the seemingly recondite errors of philosophers and the wrong turnings fatally taken by human beings at large.

Initially, it seems odd that this blend of abstract speculation and cultural critique flowed from the pen of someone who liked to stress the 'pure' character of philosophy as 'the science of Being'; to scoff at the 'St. Vitus' dance' performed by modern philosophers who manufacture 'world-views', 'all-inclusive reflection[s] on the world and... human' life (BP 5ff); and to insist, at least in his earlier writings, that his concern was not with the modern condition, but with the perennial and necessary structures of human existence. But it turns out that there can be no 'science of Being' that is not founded on an investigation of our everyday, concrete engagement with the world, and that the objection to world-view philosophizing is not to its attempts at the 'interpretation of existence and its meaning', but to its superficiality, its failure to uncover the presuppositions which make the very promulgating of world-views a possibility. And it turns out, too, that if the distressing aspects of life we now observe — its 'inauthenticity', for instance — are implicit in the human condition *per se*, they are, in modern times, manifest as never before, and for that reason ones which, at last, we can do something about, whether through our active 'resolve' or, in Heidegger's later view, through patient preparation for 'a God who can save us'.

A better clue, in fact, to the mood of Heidegger's philosophy than his characterization of it as 'pure' and 'scientific' is his endorsement of the poet Novalis' remark: 'Philosophy is authentic homesickness, a drive to be "at home" everywhere' (GA 29/309). 'At homeness' is a persistent motif in Heidegger from his early diagnosis of 'inauthentic' responses to our alienated condition to his later call for us to 'dwell' in 'the house of Being'. And it is the motif which brings philosophy and cultural critique together. 'At home' — with the world, other people and ourselves — is just what human beings are not, especially in technological modernity: and if they think they are, this is because they are 'tranquillized' and failing to confront their condition. It is the task of philosophy — or 'thinking', as he later calls it — to address and, within its limits, redress this situation. This is a task, however, in which philosophers hitherto have singularly failed. Indeed, the divisive dualisms they have constructed — subject *versus* object, mind *versus* matter, fact *versus* value, and so on — bear a heavy responsibility for the emergence of our currently 'homeless' condition.

This motif and, more generally, Heidegger's blending of philosophy with a critique of modernity, will be my main concern in the four main chapters (3-6) which follow a brief account, in Ch. 2, of Heidegger's life and the intellectual climate in which his thought took shape. Ch. 3 focuses on the earlier writings, including his most famous work, *Being and Time*, centring on his notion of our 'Being-in-the-world'. Ch. 4 discusses the notions of 'authenticity' and 'heritage' developed in those writings, and their relationship to his involvement with Nazism. By the time of that involvement, he was already beginning to develop his 'history of Being' and a critique of technology as the latest episode in that history — the topics for Ch. 5. Ch. 6 examines Heidegger's account of, and soteriological faith in, art and poetry, and his final efforts to 'think Being' in a manner freed from the shackles of a discredited philosophical tradition.

With the Collected Edition of his works planned to run to 100 volumes, some of them hefty, many of Heidegger's contributions will, unsurprisingly, receive no mention. Selection is not the only problem facing the author of a short book on Heidegger. As Grass' parody suggests, Heidegger's style is an extremely difficult one. Nouns become verbs, and vice-versa; new words are coined; old ones are used in unfamiliar senses, and then assembled into such concoctions as 'Being-already-alongside-the-world'. In the earlier writings, readers must suffer the heavyweight vocabulary of phenomenology ('ecstasis', 'categorial intuition', and the like), while some of the later work will strike them as more akin to the incantations of a mystic poet than to the essays of a professional philosopher. None of this is to deny the earthy power of the early descriptions of our everyday life or the eerie beauty of the later 'poetic thinking'. Whether the price for that beauty is, as Peter Gay remarked, that 'song [is] substituted for thought' — whether Heidegger finally became a poet rather than a thinker of our times — readers must judge for themselves.

2. Life and Context

'Aristotle was born, worked, and died'. This was how Heidegger satisfied his students' curiosity about the life of the great Greek philosopher. I shall be a little more expansive about his own life, though it was hardly a dramatically eventful one, with the notable exceptions of the year as Nazi Rector of his university and the immediate postwar years when the penalties for this episode were paid.

The son of pious Catholics, Martin Heidegger was born on 26th September 1889 at Messkirch, a small town in South-West Germany, just below the Swabian alps. He grew up only a stone's throw from the baroque church where his father, a cooper, was sexton. It was in the quiet cemetery overlooking the town that he was buried nearly ninety years later. During those years, the region was one from which he strayed only for a five-year teaching spell in Marburg and for occasional lectures abroad. Heidegger's 'rootedness' in his native soil is not, of course, unrelated either psychologically or philosophically to the motif of 'at homeness' that permeates his writings.

A church charity enabled the promising Martin to attend a *Gymnasium* and then Freiburg University as a theology student preparing for the priesthood. A weak heart scotched that ambition and Heidegger turned to philosophy, qualifying as a lecturer in 1915. Until its final months, when he served on the Western Front as a weatherman for a poison gas unit, the war did not unduly interfere with academic progress, Heidegger's main duty — for reasons of health — being that of a postal censor in Freiburg. In 1917 he married a student at Freiburg, who bore him two sons during what seems to have been a contented marriage, despite his 'special relationship', as one biographer coyly puts it, with another, better-known student, Hannah Arendt. His wife's Protestantism may have encouraged his break with Catholicism, whose 'system', he announced, he now found 'problematic and unacceptable' (Ott 106). Another reason, mooted by the more cynical, may have been Heidegger's perception that his career would then fare better with the arrival in Freiburg of the philosopher he most admired, the 'father of phenomenology', Edmund Husserl. Jewish-born, Husserl was a Protestant but, more importantly, hostile to the intrusion of religious affiliations into philosophy.

Heidegger became Husserl's *Assistent* in 1919 and, with the help of the latter's glowing testimonials ('I have not met anyone who exhibits such freshness and boundless originality' (Ott 127)), obtained a professorship in Marburg in 1923. In 1928, his great ambition was accomplished when he succeeded Husserl at Freiburg, on the strength of *Being and Time* — hurriedly published for just that purpose — and his reputation as a charismatic lecturer. Already by 1921, disgruntled colleagues had spoken of students being — as if bewitched — 'be-heideggered' (*verheideggert*).

Shortly after Hitler's accession to power in 1933, Heidegger became the *Führer* (his own designation) of a smaller domain, as Rector of his alma mater — of which more in a moment. After resigning from this position a year later, Heidegger remained teaching at Freiburg until called up to serve in a reserve unit in

1944. Released from this service, Heidegger together with some colleagues and students marched off, in an academic restaging of *Götterdämmerung*, to a remote mountain castle, there to continue lectures after Freiburg had been bombed. Brought down to earth, Heidegger was then condemned on various counts for his Nazi involvement and banned from teaching: a long-drawn out process which caused him a nervous breakdown. Partial forgiveness came in 1951 when he was made Emeritus Professor.

During his remaining years, Heidegger continued to write and lecture to packed audiences in Germany and France. Much of his time was spent at the 'mountain hut' — actually a small hillside house on the outskirts of a village — which he had had built at Todtnauberg in the 1920s. There he received a parade of admirers, not all of whom came away with their admiration increased. Sartre glumly concluded, after his visit, that his erstwhile mentor had 'gone mystical'; while Paul Celan, who had gone there 'in the hope of a word to come in my heart', left without having heard it. Despite the travails of advanced old age, Heidegger was still able until near his death to contribute prefaces to books published in his honour and to bathe in the reputation which such publications betokened, an enjoyment only partially spoiled, one imagines, by his wife's apparent tendency to tell visitors that her husband wasn't really 'that smart'. Heidegger died in Freiburg on 26th May 1976.

Until he thickened out in middle age, when he reminded Jacques Derrida of 'an old Jew from Algiers', Heidegger's features were lean and alert, his figure wiry — early photos making him look strikingly like the young A.J. Ayer, his philosophical antipode. He was kept in trim by a fondness for bucolic pastimes like wood-chopping and for skiing and handball. To the consternation of colleagues, he would sport, even at lectures, a ski-suit or an outfit resembling a peasant's 'sunday best', dubbed by his

students 'the existential suit'. These sartorial tastes squared with
his preference for sharing a bottle of Baden wine with farmers to
the company of the professoriate. Biographies to date focus too
squarely on the Rectorate, and memoirs by former students are
too awe-struck and gushing, to provide a rounded picture of
Heidegger the man. From some reports, he comes across as cold
and unsociable, though the image of the solitary mountain-sage
is an exaggerated one. Nor was he incapable of showing emo-
tion, as when 'tears welled from his eyes and choked his voice'
during his farewell lecture at Marburg.

Fairly or not, judgement on the man has come to be dictated,
almost exclusively, by the Nazi connection. After Farias' and
Ott's documentation of the depth of that connection, judgement
is likely to be harsh. 'Disturbing and frequently disgusting' is
one typical verdict on Heidegger's activities in the 1930s. Criticism has centred not only on those activities but on his subse-
quent 'cover-up' and virtual silence about the holocaust, the latter occasionally punctuated by such notoriously insensitive remarks as his comparison between the extermination camps and
the 'motorized food-industry'.

In two respects, at least, Heidegger's postwar version of his
relationship to National Socialism was accurate: his denial that
he ever subscribed to its racist ideology, and his admission that
he did at first discern the 'greatness and glory of [a] new dawn'
with the accession of Hitler (HC 94). Less reliable or downright
false are the claims that he (a) was 'beseiged' by colleagues to
become Rector of Freiburg in order to prevent the appointment
of a Party hack; (b) resisted political intrusion into the university
by, for example, opposing the 'cleansing laws' directed against
Jews; (c) protected Jewish lecturers; (d) was never an active
Party member; (e) resigned as Rector because of opposition to
his reforms from both faculty and Party; (f) was anyway totally

disillusioned with the Nazis by 1934; and (g) was later, because of his criticisms of the regime, put under surveillance by the authorities who then tried to get rid of him in 1944 by drafting him into a *Volkssturm* unit.

A more accurate account is this. Heidegger was not dragooned as Rector, but the willing candidate of a clique of Nazi sympathizers. Far from opposing political interference, it was his goal 'from the very first day', according to a letter, to change the University 'in accordance with... the demands of the National Socialist State' (Sheehan 39). While he did defend retention of some Jewish lecturers, on grounds of international image, he refused to supervise Jewish students, denounced one lecturer for his Jewish associations, and failed to come to Husserl's aid when his old mentor fell foul of the anti-Jewish laws. (The shoddy treatment of Husserl had a longer history. In 1923, when he owed his very livelihood to Husserl's support, Heidegger could write to a friend, 'Husserl has completely lost his marbles — if he was ever "all there" to start with' (Ott 182). In 1938, he stayed away from Husserl's funeral, and later dropped the dedication to Husserl from a new edition of *Being and Time*). His support for the Party was very real, its calibre apparent from such public statements as this, in support of Hitler's plebiscite on leaving the League of Nations: 'Th[e] future is bound to the *Führer*. In choosing this future, the people cannot... vote Yes without also including in this Yes the *Führer* and the political movement... pledged unconditionally to him' (HC 48). Heidegger did not resign in 1934 at the behest of the Party, but out of disappointment at his failure to reorganize the University as he wished. Nor did his allegiance to the Party end in that year. To an ex-student in 1936, he admitted his continuing 'engagement', and even later still occasionally made admiring references to Hitler in lectures. Although out of favour, mainly for reasons of professional jealousy, with the Party's ideological hacks, Heidegger was never seriously considered to be a dissident.

For some critics, of course, Heidegger stands condemned irrespective of the 'disgusting' episodes and his cover-up. If he was a sincere Nazi, he is damned, and if he wasn't, then he must have been an unscrupulous opportunist. Heidegger's defence was threefold. First, he was not 'so wise' and 'prophetic' as others — who then waited ten years before doing anything — to foresee the disaster National Socialism would become (R 486). Second, if more 'capable' people, like himself, had worked within the movement instead of remaining aloof, that disaster just might have been averted. Finally, there really was in 1933 — in Hitler's vision, if not that of his followers — the glimmer of 'a new dawn' and a certain 'inner truth'. With this final plea entered, the focus shifts from personal involvement with a political party to the relationship of a philosophy with a political ideology. I postpone discussion of this relationship to Ch. 4.

It was during the years immediately following the 1914-18 war, the Weimar years, that the interests which would occupy Heidegger for the rest of his life assumed definite shape. Someone as keen as he was to emphasize the historical situatedness of a thinker would hardly deny the role played in this crystallization of his thought by the context — intellectual, cultural, and political — of his times.

Thanks to Kurt Weil, Christopher Isherwood and other witnesses, our images of the Weimar years are rich and lively. Various images compete: that of a dizzy society of unbooted experimentation in both the arts and lifestyles; that of whistling young *Wanderer* escaping the cities for the fresh air of the Black Forest; and that of sinister, violent undercurrents building up to a flood. The shameless legs of Sally Bowles or Marlene Dietrich juxtapose with the jackbooted ones of the 'Brownshirts'. Sometimes the images coalesce, as when in the film *Cabaret* golden-haired boys and girls at a country inn break into a Nazi song. In a sense, perhaps, the images do not compete, for each attests to the rejection — whether by way of devil-may-care apathy, escapism, or outright hostility — of the bourgeois, democratic, industrialized Germany that politicians were striving to forge in the wake of national humiliation.

I return to these aspects of the Weimar period in a moment, after briefly sketching the philosophical currents which reflected in variety and antagonism those of the wider culture. Since the demise by the middle of the nineteenth century of the great systems of idealism, a main tendency in German philosophy had been towards various forms of naturalism — materialism, psychologism and positivism (soon to receive radical expression, over the border, in the Logical Positivism of the Vienna Circle). By 'naturalism' I mean the conviction that it is the empirical sciences alone which are the proper vehicles of knowledge. Even the truths of logic and mathematics can, according to psychologism, be treated as descriptions of the empirically testable workings of the human mind.

It was on the adequacy or otherwise of naturalism that debate during the period which concerns us focussed. At least three schools of thought rebelled against this tendency. First, there were the *Lebensphilosophen*, for whom the fundamental and all-embracing concept in the understanding of at least human life — that of life itself — is not amenable to ordinary scientific investigation. Wilhelm Dilthey had already referred to the 'conflict between the tendencies of life and the goal of science', arguing that investigation of human life required a mode of understanding, *Verstehen*, and a style of interpretation quite foreign to the natural sciences. Less cool heads, like Oswald Spengler and Ludwig Klages, were insisting that irrational intuition and 'thinking with the blood' were the only means of grasping life, not the 'chemical and static' methods of science. Second, there were the proponents of 'world-view' philosophizing, such as the young Karl Jaspers. Naturalism, on this approach, is right to hold that the claims of religion and various metaphysical systems cannot be rationally secured. But then naturalism is itself just one more world-view constructed to make sense of reality and human existence — and not, perhaps, a satisfying one given its silence over the realm of morality. The only task of the philosopher can be to present alternative world-views, by all means making his own preference clear, but finally leaving it to his readers to decide which they find most palatable.

Despite his references to 'world-views philosophers' as superficial and to the 'philosophers of life' as 'higher journalists', Heidegger was sympathetic to the concerns and the anti-naturalism of both schools. The former were right to castigate naturalism for its incapacity to address issues of meaning and value, as were the latter in recognizing that human life must be explored by methods very different from those of the natural sciences. The proper response, however, need not be abandonment of rational thought, whether by treating all philosophical systems as so many world-views to 'choose' between or by postulating some 'biological' force, life, accessible only to gut intuition.

It was the third of the critical responses to naturalism, phenomenology, which inspired Heidegger's own position. 'Illumined by the phenomenological attitude', he recalls, 'I was brought to the path of the question of Being' (TB 80). As a young student, he already accepted Husserl's case against the psychologistic treatment of logic and mathematics, part of a wider dismissal of naturalism in which Heidegger came to concur. For Husserl, positivist philosophy had made itself 'contemptible' by taking empirical science as the repository of fundamental knowledge.

This it cannot be, since the study of 'everything contingent' pre-supposes a grasp of the 'essences' of the things studied. To this examination of the 'meanings' of the things science studies, sci-ence itself can contribute nothing. Indeed, it is a distraction, so that we need to 'bracket' or 'put out of play' all scientific dis-coveries in order to focus on essences or meanings. This return to the 'absolute beginnings' or presuppositions of knowledge is phenomenology, which, as Husserl explains in *Ideas I*, is there-fore not 'a science of facts', but an enquiry into 'essential be-ing... which aims exclusively at establishing "knowledge of es-sences"'. Heidegger will radically depart from Husserl's own execution of phenomenology's programme, but not from the conviction that the empirical sciences' account of things is de-rivative from something more fundamental, nor from the sense that the truly 'pressing question' for philosophy is the 'whence and how' of our capacity to experience things in the first place.

It may seem a big jump from phenomenology's critique of naturalism and positivism to the failure of the Weimar Republic to secure popular allegiance — a failure evidenced by the frivol-ity, escapism and violence mentioned above. But to its critics, naturalism was never a mere intellectual error, for the attitude it represented bore a heavy responsibility for 'the tragedy of cul-ture' which right-wing thinkers saw enacted in Germany. For Dilthey, it contributed to a mechanistic view of the world as 'something other [and] alien' to ourselves; or, as Husserl put it, to a dualistic picture of 'nature... alien to spirit'.

The notion of *Kultur* resonated strongly in the 1920s, and was contrasted with that of *Zivilisation*. For Spengler, 'the de-cline of the West' was due to erosion of the culture of nordic 'Faustian man' by civilization: the replacement of cultural im-peratives — community, the will of a *Volk*, hardness and danger — by a civilized ideology of individualism, cosmopolitanism,

comfort and security. The drift to the cities, democracy, trade
unions, modernism in the arts, and other favourite bugbears of
the Right were so many ingredients in the demise of traditional
culture, leaving men and women rootless and frightened. None
of these developments would have been possible, it was charged,
except for the gradual victory of the perverted Enlightenment
ideal of detached, disengaged theoretical reason. The bitter fruit
of this victory was naturalism's elevation of science as the arbiter of truth and of mere utility as the arbiter of morality. It was
this victory, Max Weber famously lamented, which had produced
a 'disenchanted' world in which to live — as 'grey' and 'spec-
tre-like' as the one which Goethe had charged his Enlightenment
contemporaries with concocting — and had reduced reason to a
calculating 'purposive rationality'.

Heidegger was impressed by — and indeed helped to forge
— this thesis of the complicity of naturalism in 'the tragedy of
culture', in the 'homelessness', 'levelling', 'averageness', and
'deep boredom' of the times. This *Schwarzwald* redneck', as
Richard Rorty dubs him, was indeed a 'traditionalist'. 'I know
that everything... great originated from the fact that man had a
home and was rooted in a tradition' (HC 106). His main debt,
however, was not to such romantic reactionaries as Moeller van
den Bruck and Stefan George, with their rejection of 'Satanic'
technology and their call for a 'Third Reich' which would inherit
the mantle of the mediaeval Hohenzollern empire. It was, rather,
to the aptly named 'reactionary modernists', writers who 'succeeded in incorporating technology into the symbolism and language of *Kultur*... by taking it out of the realm of *Zivilisation*'
(Herf 16). It was not that Heidegger ever shared Spengler's conviction that technology is the highest expression of 'Faustian
man's' will-to-power, or Ernst Jünger's 'deep piety' towards
machines and their engineers. But neither his enthusiasm for the

Nazis, his 'history of Being', nor the hopes he invested in a 'saving power', are intelligible without recognizing the depth of his belief, inherited from these authors, that technology is the essential dimension of modernity, a 'metaphysical power' which impresses its 'stamp' or *Gestalt* on our times.

3. Being-in-the-World

Philosophy, detractors charge, never progresses. 'How do we know there is an external world?', 'How are mind and body related?', and other favourite questions are never answered to everyone's satisfaction. Long-forgotten solutions suddenly get resurrected, only to be reburied a few Journal issues later. Is this because such questions are too complicated for even the cleverest mind, because philosophers are not very clever, or what? Heidegger and Wittgenstein owe much of their importance to their diagnosis of philosophy's failure to make progress. This is due, they argue, not to the depth or complexity of the questions posed, but to the ways they are posed. What the questions deserve is not new solutions, but dissolution or 'deconstruction', as do the frameworks of thought which generate them. We have, says Heidegger, 'fallen prey' to a certain tradition, whose basic tenets have come to seem 'self-evident' and into which philosophy has 'deteriorated' (BT 43f). We cannot, however, ignore this tradition and start afresh, partly because it does contain genuine insights, partly because we are too much in thrall to its concepts and vocabulary to step outside of it 'just like that'. More importantly, the tradition continues and 'hardens' tendencies of ordinary thought which, though misguided, have their source in genuine, unarticulated understanding. If we are to recapture and articulate that understanding, the tradition must be 'loosened-up', 'deconstructed down to the sources' it draws upon (BP 23). True vision requires correction of a skewed one.

The tradition to which we have fallen prey is the Cartesian one. Though later thinkers, like Kant and Husserl, have departed from Descartes in important respects, theirs are still detours, in Heidegger's view, within the general framework erected by 'the father of modern philosophy'. The three elements of Descartes' framework which Heidegger intends to reject are his accounts of the external world, the mind, and the relation between the two. The distinctive thesis of 'modern philosophy' is that 'the basic ways of Being are the Being of Nature (*res extensa*) and the Being of Mind *(res cogitans)*' (BP 122). In one corner, there stands nature, reality, the world — conceived of as an aggregate of material objects whose essential properties are spatial. This conception was encouraged by the science of Descartes' day and has since nurtured the conviction that the world is one which mathematical physics is preeminently 'well-suited to grasp' (BT 129). In the other corner are minds or 'thinking things' — unextended mental entities defined by thought and self-consciousness. 'Transparent' to itself, the mind is something whose nature and operations are primarily to be grasped through introspection.

Descartes' account of existence, his ontology, is therefore one of 'substances', a substance being defined as an entity which 'needs no other entity in order to exist'. If material objects and minds needed something else, or one another, they would not be substances, nor therefore the basic kinds of entity Descartes holds them to be. For Descartes, to be sure, such entities are created by God, and there are contingent, causal connections between them. Still, body and mind can be conceived of independently both of God and of one another, and are in that — the relevant — sense independent, with no logical requirement that any other

entity exist. There just might, in that sense, never have existed
anything other than that tree or my mind.

As it happens, Descartes himself was convinced that things
outside my mind do exist, including my body which 'interacts'
with my mind. My arm moves because I will it to; I get depressed
because of my acne. Here, famously, Descartes generates a problem. How could such radically different kinds of substance, mental
and physical, interact or, as Heidegger puts it, be 'welded' together? Some philosophers within the Cartesian tradition thought
they could not, that mind and body merely operate in parallel,
thanks to God's engineering, so that it is only *as if* they influence
one another. Despite such differences, the tradition agrees on
the basic relation between the two kinds of substance, as one
between 'subjects' and 'objects', with the former 'representing'
to themselves the objects which 'stand over against' them.
Whether these representations — perceptions, say — present
objects 'directly' or only *via* such intermediaries as mental images, is a moot point. What is not disputed is that representation
is our basic relation to the world, since I can only do other things
— like moving my arm or getting depressed over my acne — if
I can first represent to myself how things are. This, of course,
raises a further problem: how do I *know* that any of my representations are correct? Assuming that I do, we could redescribe the
basic relation to the world as 'knowing'. For the tradition, writes
Heidegger, 'knowing the world' is the 'single exemplar' of our
essential relation to it (BT 86).

Heidegger's attempt to fit nearly all philosophers since
Descartes into a single framework is surely Procrustean. Either
the framework has to be stretched or the stature of various
thinkers shrunk. Take Kant, who departs from Descartes at several
crucial points. Minds, for Kant, are not composed of some 'mind-
stuff'. Nor are they logically isolated from the world, since objects

cannot be conceived of independently from ourselves, being experienced only under conditions, like those of space and time, which *we* impose. Be that as it may, Heidegger insists that it is 'only in semblance' that Kant has 'given up a Cartesian approach of positing a subject one can come across in isolation' from the world (BT 248), and that Kant's world remains a Cartesian one of 'persistent objects' in space, fully describable in Newtonian physics. Perhaps we should not become unduly taxed by how 'Cartesian' Kant and other thinkers have been. Most of Heidegger's main criticisms of Descartes apply to them as well.

Why, according to Heidegger, does the Cartesian tradition need 'destroying'? Certainly there is the pragmatic motive of thereby dissolving the 'unsolvable' questions about our knowledge of the external world and the 'interaction' between mind and body to which that tradition gives rise. But enticing as the burials of 'the problem of knowledge' and 'the mind-body problem' are, this is not a reason for rejecting the tradition. After all, if that tradition is well-founded, such problems just won't stay buried. Those looking to Heidegger for sharp, knockdown arguments against the tradition will be disappointed. He tells us, to be sure, that the traditional perspective is superficial, taking as 'first and closest to us' notions which are in fact highly derivative, such as that of a 'mere' physical object or that of 'representing' the world. And he complains that it fails to grasp things in their necessary, holistic interconnections. But to agree with him, we need to have appreciated Heidegger's own depiction of our basic relation to the world and his explanation of why philosophers have been made blind to this. As Heidegger himself stresses, the 'deconstruction' of the tradition necessarily 'belongs together' with, and 'receives grounding' in, the 'construction' of an alternative (BP 23).

Before turning to that 'construction', we need to identify the most general defect Heidegger discerns in the traditional perspective. What is really 'messing up' philosophy, he wrote in 1919, is 'not just naturalism... but the... dominance and primacy of the *theoretical*' (GA 56/7 87). What Heidegger means by this term is not the production of theories, but a prerequisite for this: disengagement from practical concerns in favour of disinterested observation and 'spectating'. It is this disengaged theoretical stance philosophers have traditionally striven to adopt. Husserl, for instance, is only aping Descartes in demanding a 'deliberate *epoche* ('abstention') from all practical interests' so as to become a 'non-participating spectator'. 'The dominance of the theoretical' is pernicious, Heidegger holds, because it ignores that mode of understanding the world implicit in the engaged stance of agents with 'practical interests'. 'By looking at the world theoretically we have already dimmed it down to the uniformity of what is purely present-at-hand (*vorhanden*)' (BT 177) — of what is 'just there' before us, a mere 'thing of nature' to be observed, like a plant by a botanist. From this theoretical stance, it is a short hop to the Cartesian vision of the world as a collection of extended substances and of ourselves as just 'thinking things' representing that world to ourselves.

Although the theoretical stance is very different from people's everyday, engaged one, Heidegger argues that it is one we all have a powerful tendency to adopt once we pause from our practices and stop to reflect on things. Ironically, this is because we are, for the most part, so thoroughly engaged. Absorbed in an activity, I 'dwell alongside' the objects, like hammers, which figure in it, to the exclusion of self-conscious concern with the goal of the activity. When I pause and take stock, perhaps because the nail won't go in, it is the hammer as a 'mere' physical object — a lump of wood joined to a piece of metal — that is salient for me, not the project of building a shed in which the hammer has its role. I stop and stare, and scientists and philosophers who screen out 'practical interests' are, therefore, only continuing in a sophisticated way what we all tend to do when taking reflective stock. Hence, the 'neglects' of the Cartesian tradition are not mere '"mistakes" which can be easily corrected', but have their roots in a 'power' or tendency to which all of us are 'condemned' (HCT 131).

Heidegger variously expresses what is required for the Cartesian perspective to be corrected. He demands, first, a reversal of the 'modern' priority of epistemology over ontology — of enquiries into knowledge over ones into existence. Knowledge 'in the usual spectator sense... presupposes existence' (BP 276), since no account of knowledge is possible without a prior understanding of the nature of knowers and what they know. The crucial issue is begged when it is assumed that we are simply 'thinking things' confronted by extended ones, the only problem then being how we escape from our 'inner spheres' so as to acquire knowledge about these external objects.

A second, related reversal Heidegger demands is the move from 'the consideration of beings [entities] to the... thematization of Being' (BP 227). This is the kind of statement from which Oxford lecturers wanted their students protected. But in the writings which presently concern us, nothing mysterious is intended by 'the question of Being' which it is the stated task of *Being and Time* to address. 'Being' is glossed as 'that on the basis of which entities are already understood' (BT 25-6). Being, Heidegger immediately adds, is not itself an entity, not even a very impressive one like God. It is always what entities, like you or your pen, have. To move from 'the consideration of beings' to their Being is, in practice, to enquire into the underlying conditions for their being encountered, their 'showing up' for us, at all: an enquiry passed over, Heidegger believes, in the Cartesian tradition. In *Being and Time*, which was never completed, very little in fact is said about Being in general, but a great deal about the Being of particular kinds of entity, such as artifacts and people. We won't go far wrong if we construe Heidegger as investigating the conditions for the intelligibility of these kinds of entity, as trying to 'make sense of our ability to make sense of things' (Dreyfus 10).

Finally, Heidegger tells us that philosophy must become phenomenology. He takes issue with Husserl, 'the father of phenomenology', on several counts, but with the spirit and broad strategy of his mentor he is in harmony. Husserl's admirable rallying-cry was 'Back to the things [matters, *Sachen*] themselves!': that is, we must free ourselves from metaphysical and scientific preconceptions and let things 'show' themselves to us as they are, unobstructed by distorting prisms. In the phrase '"show" themselves to us as they are', moreover, is implied the proper strategy for philosophy, one recognized but, thinks Heidegger, wrongly executed by Husserl. Since things show themselves to us, it is with us that enquiry into their Being — the conditions for their being encountered and understood — must begin. We already 'understand something like Being' (BT 39). Hence to uncover structures of intelligibility must be a matter of teasing out an understanding which, however inchoately, each of us has. This is why 'fundamental ontology' and phenomenology must be pursued *via* an 'analytic of *Dasein* [Heidegger's name for our kind of Being]'. Next, since things show themselves *as* this or that, our primary encounter with them is interpretative: we are, necessarily, traffickers in meaning. Hence, the kind of understanding on which to focus in order to articulate the Being of anything is 'hermeneutic': understanding in the shape of interpreting rather than, say, of ascertaining causes and effects.

Stitching together these recipes for correcting the Cartesian perspective, we obtain Heidegger's definition of proper philosophy: 'phenomenological ontology [which] takes its departure from a hermeneutic of *Dasein*' (BT 62). We can now proceed to this point of departure, the account of our Being-in-the-world which is to serve as the 'guiding-line' for the enquiry into Being in general.

The hyphens indicate that Being-in-the-world is a 'unitary phenomenon', whose 'constitutive items' — the world, ourselves, and our 'being-in' it — can at best be provisionally distinguished (BT 78). A complete account of one would be a complete account of the others, and we must resist the Cartesian temptation to think we are dealing here with independent entities — us and the world — which, as it happens, are somehow wired together. Thus we should be clear from the start that 'being-in' is not a spatial relationship. I am not 'in-the-world' as a pea in a pod, but more in the sense that someone is in the world of motor-racing or fashion. It is a matter of engagement, not location. Heidegger also emphasizes from the start that the part of his account which concerns us in this chapter addresses our 'average everyday' Being-in-the-world. Not only are less 'average' aspects of human existence 'founded' on this, but it is the understanding implicit in everyday life which is least cluttered up by theory and the most suitable, therefore, to serve as the 'source' from which to draw if the 'hardened tradition' of philosophy and science is to be 'loosened-up'.

In everyday life, things are not initially or 'proximally' encountered by us as mere objects present-at-hand through pure 'perceptual cognition'. Rather, we experience them as 'ready-to-hand' (*zuhanden*) — as functional, 'manipulable' items like hammers and pens which figure in a field of 'concern': and we do so through our practical 'dealings' with them, not through disengaged observation. Heidegger calls the 'entities which we encounter in concern "equipment" (*Zeuge*)' (BT 97). Two pos-

sible misunderstandings are quickly scotched. Although our dealings with equipment are contrasted with 'knowledge in the usual
spectator sense', they are not mindless manipulations like those
of dung-beetles. 'Coping' with equipment 'has its own kind of
"knowledge"', an intelligent know-how, so it is not that we first
deal with things blindly and only later, when reflecting, recognize what they are and what we are doing with them. On the
contrary, it is through hammering that a hammer is revealed as
what it is. Second, it is not only hammers and similar artifacts
which are encountered as ready-to-hand. Nature, too, is not initially experienced as just there, present-at-hand. 'The wood is a
forest of timber' and even the south wind is first 'discovered in
its Being' — as a sign of rain, say — through activities like farming (BT 100, 112).

It is not a mere empirical fact that we first encounter things in
the world as ready-to-hand. Unless we did so, we could not then
'make accessible what is just present-at-hand' (BT 122). For
unless things are first 'lit up' in virtue of the roles they play within
our practical concerns, nothing would stand out for us to then
'stare' at and submit to 'perceptual cognition'. The lacuna in the
Cartesian tradition is its failure to ask how the extended things
we represent to ourselves should ever have emerged as
discriminable items for perceptual attention. The traditional question 'How do we know things?' is insufficiently basic, for it presupposes a prior mode of access to them, the practical dealings
which enable things to 'show up'. Experiencing things as present-
at-hand is necessarily derivative from, 'later than', this 'proximal' encounter with them. In fact, we only switch to observing
things present-at-hand when something goes wrong in our everyday dealings with equipment. Only when the hammer malfunc-
tions does it become 'conspicuous' as a mere physical object, a
fusion of wood and metal which we now need to inspect in ab-

straction from its usual functional role. Descartes' mistake was to take this parasitic spectatorial stance towards the object as the primary one, and then to identify the 'real' object with this 'dimmed down' lump of extended matter. One may as well insist that a symphony is 'really' just some vibrations in the air.

It may sound strained to call trees and winds ready-to-hand equipment for, despite being usable by carpenters and sailors, these uses surely do not define them. Heidegger's point is that such entities, even if not equipment strictly speaking, first get 'lit up' for us through their involvement with what is, literally, equipment. Even when the forest and wind are not being put to use, they enter into our practical concerns as 'signs', as when the south wind presages the rain which threatens the crops. More generally, 'our concern discovers nature as having a certain direction' relevant to our projects (BT 100).

We have here touched on two important and related aspects of the world we are 'in': holism and meaningfulness. Taken strictly, Heidegger writes, there is no such thing as '*an* equipment', since each item necessarily belongs within a totality. Typically, indeed, it is not this or that item individually, the planks and the saw, say, which one initially experiences, but a whole, the workshop, for example. Nor is the involvement of items with one another and with ourselves primarily a matter of causal connections. Rather, it is a one of 'references or assignments' (BT 105). It is not that everything ready-to-hand is, strictly, a sign in the manner of, say, a car's indicator. Still, all of it is 'sign-like' in that it 'points' or 'refers' to something beyond itself. The saw is in order to cut the plank, which goes towards making the table, which is for the sake of the people who will eat off it. It is in virtue of relations like 'in order to', 'towards' and 'for the sake of' that ready-to-hand items have their identity, an identity always within a 'referential totality'.

The example of the table shows that such equipmental wholes as a lumber-mill, a workshop and the house for which the table is destined cannot be understood in isolation from one another. Each 'refers' to the others. It follows that everything ready-to-hand belongs to a single 'relational totality'. It is this grand 'structural whole of meaningful connections' (HCT 209-10) that Heidegger calls 'the world'. Only though first being engaged in the world, so construed, can one then — through prescinding from that engagement — arrive at that thin and 'dimmed down' conception of the world as composed of a senseless 'world-stuff', *res extensa,* the world which the Cartesian tradition takes our abode to be. That the world is a totality of 'significance', imbued as it were by *logos,* has important implications, we will see, for the nature of our 'being-in' it and our understanding of it. To appreciate those implications, Heidegger's conception of the we who are in-the-world must first be sketched.

Heidegger is reluctant to call us by such familiar epithets as 'people'. Instead he borrows a common German word, *Dasein,* meaning 'being' or 'existence', to refer both to 'the manner of Being which... man... possesses' and to the creatures which possess it (BT 32). It is not excluded that non-human creatures should have *Dasein,* Martians perhaps or, though Heidegger doubts it, some higher animals. His coyness about the familiar epithets registers a determination to ignore biological and other 'irrelevant' features of human beings which such epithets are likely to suggest.

We are introduced to *Dasein,* our kind of Being, in fairly uncontentious, if oddly expressed, ways. To begin with, *Dasein* is 'in each case mine' (BT 67), which means that each of us not merely has that kind of Being, but can own to it, lay claim to it. Second, *Dasein* is such that Being, *its* Being especially, is 'an issue for it'. We not only care about ourselves and things in an obvious enough way, but about the *kind* of creatures we have the capacity to makes ourselves into. In both respects we differ from mere physical objects and, in the latter, from animals as well. Heidegger soon proceeds, however, to say some distinctly puzzling things about *Dasein*. Only *Dasein* 'exists' and it exists as 'its there': it is 'beyond itself' and 'is its possibility'. Stranger still, *Dasein* is 'its clearing (*Lichtung*)' and 'its disclosedness [or 'laid-openness', *Erschlossenheit*]' (BT 169ff, BP 300). What are we to make of all this? The claim that only *Dasein* 'exists' plays on the etymology of the word, derived from the Latin *ex-stare* (to 'stand out from') and is of a piece, therefore, with the claim that *Dasein*'s Being (*Sein*) is 'its there [*da*]'.

A main purpose of Heidegger's bizarre characterizations is to drive home that *Dasein* 'does not have the kind of Being [of] something merely present-at-hand' (BT 43), nor of something merely ready-to-hand. The target here is the Cartesian construal of human being 'in the very same way as the Being of *res extensa*' (BT 98), as if people were 'things', albeit composed of a different stuff endowing them with rather special properties. The crucial error in this is not so much the postulating of a special 'soul-stuff' but the one, also committed by Kant and Husserl, of treating *Dasein* as an object, however 'pure', to be distinguished from what it does, as an 'ego-pole' from which thoughts and actions somehow 'radiate' (BP 158). Thus, *Dasein* does not *have* possibilities open to it as a bonus added to its existence: it *is* its possibilities in that no sense can be made of a person's existence except in terms of the projects, out of the many available, upon which he is engaged. *Dasein* is to be compared less with a source of light, an 'ego-pole', than with the light itself. Light is not an object which illuminates things: it *is* the illumination. And it is always 'beyond', 'ahead' or 'out there', wherever the things illuminated are. Light is a 'clearing' where things show themselves, a region 'laid open' for them to appear in. Analogously, *Dasein* is not an object which happens to 'disclose' other objects in its neighbourhood. Rather, it exists in and through its disclosure of the world, its 'concernful' engagement or 'meaningful connection' with it.

The larger point, then, to Heidegger's strange characterizations of *Dasein* is to insist that it is not a kind of substance, something that 'needs no other entity in order to be'. Without objects there to reflect it, there is no light: it needs them in order to illuminate, to be light at all. *Dasein*, similarly, needs the world as much as the world, as 'significance', needs it. They need one another in the strong sense that neither can be conceived in the other's absence. 'Self and the world belong together... [They] are not two beings, like subject and object', but 'the unity of Being-in-the-world' (BP 297). To be anything, an object must be 'lit up' for us in a structure of significance: and to be anything, we must be engaged in the world as creatures who light it up.

Since *Dasein* is so intimately related to its world, little can be said about it in abstraction from this relation. Still, two important points about *Dasein* should be made before we proceed to elaborate that relation. The first concerns self-knowledge. Predictably, Heidegger rejects the Cartesian model of introspective awareness of a transparent 'inner' sphere, the *cogito*. Self-reflection is indeed possible, but this is not a matter of a self as subject seeing into itself as a transparent object. For one thing, 'extravagant grubbing about in one's soul can be... counterfeit... or pathologically eccentric' (BP 160). More important, no 'espionage on the ego' is necessary for self-knowledge. The shoemaker who wants to understand himself, what 'makes him tick', looks around him — at his workshop, his family, and so on. For it is from what he is involved in that his 'own self' is reflected back to him. *Dasein* 'finds itself primarily in things', those that constitute the world of its concern. Since 'each of us is what he pursues and cares for', we understand ourselves through understanding our world (BP 159-60). Without the latter, there would be nothing for armchair introspection to gaze into.

There is a further vehicle of self-knowledge — other people, in whose eyes I am, so to speak, reflected. This leads to a second crucial feature of *Dasein*: it is necessarily 'Being-with-others'. The spectre of solipsism which haunts the Cartesian tradition is therefore dispelled from the outset. I do not first encounter the world and then 'add on in thought' the presence of other creatures like myself. Rather, in encountering things in the world, such as clothes and fields, other people are encountered too, even if they are not physically present — the potential wearer of the clothes, the owner of the land, and so on. Ready-to-hand items have an 'essential reference' to people, for they can be the items they are only in relation to their users, makers, wearers, or whatever (BT 153ff). To speculate with Descartes that I am alone is, therefore, to imagine away the world itself.

But how do I *know* there are 'minds' behind the wearers of the clothes, the workers in the field? The question is a bad one. Precisely because I encounter them at work, play and the like, it is guaranteed that they, too, are *Dasein*, intelligent agents. Were I a private 'inner' sphere, accessible only to introspection, I could indeed wonder if 'inside' those at work and play there is anything similar to what I discover in myself. But I am not that: I am *Dasein*, which 'finds "itself" in what it does, uses, expects, avoids' (BT 155). And this is just the way I 'find' others as well. Just as, 'proximally', I encounter things through 'concern', not 'perceptual cognition', so it is through a practical 'solicitude' that I first encounter other people. (Like 'concern', 'solicitude' can exist in 'deficient' modes, such as not giving a damn about one's neighbours).

So pervasive in everyday life is one's Being-with-others that it can 'dissolve one's own *Dasein*', rendering one virtually anonymous. Thus in many contexts, as at a football match or on a bus, I do not distinguish myself from others. It is *we* who applaud the goal, *we* who are squashed up reading *our* newspaper. Heidegger, indeed, goes further: 'the Self of everyday *Dasein* is the they-self' (BT 167). 'Formally', of course, we can be individuated as I, you, she and so on: but in practice it is we or they — the unspecified 'public' — which has taken over the roles usually accredited to a self, such as exercizing 'dominion' over behaviour or interpreting things. We are clearly moving here from a mere 'analytic' of human existence to an appraisal of the human condition, as one in which people get 'levelled down' and 'disburdened' of their 'authentic' individuality. This is a topic for Ch. 4.

Inevitably, given the unitary nature of *Dasein*'s Being-in-the-world, something has already been gleaned from the discussions of *Dasein* and the world about the relation of 'being-in'. We know, for example, that a person is not 'in' an environment *qua* geographical region, but as a field of 'concern'. What has so far been gleaned is lacking, however, in detail, depth, and unity. Take, for instance, the intelligent know-how which marks our 'proximal' encounter with things. We need to know more about this, what 'grounds' it, and how it connects up with, say, the claim that our Being is an 'issue' for us. These lacks are made good in Heidegger's proposal that 'care [*Sorge*]' is *Dasein*'s way of Being-in-the-world. Care at once 'grounds' and draws together various aspects of *Dasein* and the world, while the detail so far missing is supplied by describing the components in the structure of care. With the account of care, we grasp — almost, at least — how it is possible for anything to 'show up' for us, and hence for there to be both a world and *Dasein*.

'Care', needless to say, is used in a special sense, for it is not Heidegger's point that we are always worrying about things or caring for them like a hen for her brood. In Heidegger's sense, carefreeness and indifference belong to care as much as do worry and motherly love. Care, and so *Dasein*'s Being, is defined in inimitable Heideggerese as 'ahead-of-itself-Being-already-in-(the-world) as Being-alongside (entities encountered within-the-world)' (BT 237). The components in this definition — 'ahead-of', 'already-in' and 'alongside' — pair off with *Dasein*'s three essential components (or 'existentialia') of 'understanding', 'situatedness' (*Befindlichkeit*) and 'fallenness'. Only for a creature who understands or is 'ahead-of', who is situated or 'already-in', and who is fallen or 'alongside', can things and the world 'show up'. Only such a creature is *Dasein*.

Let me try to unpack Heidegger's notion of care and the peculiar vocabulary invoked. 'Proximally', recall, we encounter things as ready-to-hand equipment, and do so through unreflective, yet intelligent dealings with them. Only as 'absorbed' in activities and equipment do we first encounter things. It is this 'being absorbed in the world' which Heidegger calls 'being-alongside' things, and to describe *Dasein* as 'fallen' means primarily that it is 'for the most part alongside the "world" of its concern' (BT 80, 220). In short, I am 'fallen' or 'alongside' things as absorbed in dealing with them. Nor, of course, am I absorbed alone: my 'fallenness' is also an 'absorption in Being-with-one-another'. My dealings are 'guided' by public practices and are with things already interpreted through those practices. Even such an eccentric loner's hobby as decorating dog-ends presupposes the socially intelligible practices of smoking and decorating. Hence 'fallenness', 'being-alongside' things, attests to what Heidegger calls 'thrownness': *Dasein*'s being, at any time, 'delivered over' to a world already mapped out for it by public practices and understanding.

'Thrownness' is one aspect of the 'factical' situation which *Dasein* always finds itself 'already-in', a situation disclosed to *Dasein* by what I called 'situatedness'. Situatedness involves an attunement to a range of available activities and projects: the appreciation, say, by a contemporary Englishman that the way of *bushido* is not an option for him. It includes, as well, 'moods' or attitudes towards the world that are prerequisite for seeing things in ways relevant to action. In 'bad moods', for example, the world can appear as burdensome, and this will affect both what one might become engaged in and how. Finally, it is in *Dasein*'s situatedness that the 'sort of thing [that] can "matter" to it is grounded' (BT 176). In our kind of culture, for example, illness and old age are feared, rather than taken for granted: hence they 'matter', and are perceived as threatening, things 'to do something about'. What these dimensions of situatedness have in common is their revealing to us aspects of our circumstances, of 'where we are at', which bear on the actions and stances we may take. (The word 'situation' in Heidegger's writings refers not to a mere state of affairs, but to what motivates and calls for a stance to be adopted. See GA 56/7 205ff). Indeed, it is what is disclosed in situatedness that 'makes it possible first of all to direct oneself towards something' (BT 176), to become absorbed in this or that. Stripped of an attunement to the situation we are 'thrown' into, of 'moods', and of any sense of things 'mattering', we would be paralysed. In Heideggerese, unless we were 'already-in' the world, we could never draw 'alongside' it.

We would be equally paralysed, however, if being 'already-in' and 'alongside' exhausted our existence. More accurately, we could not enjoy those relations to the world unless we stood to it in the further one of being 'ahead' of ourselves in the world.

We met with this and kindred terms earlier, interpreting their point as emphasizing that *Dasein* is 'out there', engaged in the world. But Heidegger soon gives 'ahead-of' a more temporal sense: *Dasein* is 'ahead-of-itself' in being directed 'towards [its] potentiality-for-Being', towards what it will or might become, the possibilities 'for the sake of which' it acts (BT 236f). There are two reasons why *Dasein* must be 'ahead-of-itself'. First, even if we are attuned to the circumstances in which we are thrown, dealing with them would be either impossible or a matter of mere automatic response without a sense of the possibilities open to us and, more generally, of the kind of creatures we want to be. Without such a sense, attunement — in the shape of fear, say — could not motivate actions, ways of being 'alongside' things. Second, and more critically, nothing could genuinely 'show up' for us and therefore figure as something to deal with, were we not directed towards our future possibilities. This is because for anything to 'show up' or be disclosed to us, it must be understood as this or that. *Dasein*'s dealings with things, though typically unreflective, are intelligent, not the blind, mechanical doings of a robot or insect. Hence they involve understanding, and whatever is 'disclosed in understanding... is accessible in such a way that its "as which" structure can be made to stand out' (BT 189). Understanding something *as* something, however, presupposes just that directedness which constitutes *Dasein*'s being 'ahead-of-itself'. Only in the light of 'projecting' my actions, and the things with which I deal, upon the future possibilities 'for the sake of which' we live as we do, can anything be understood as this or that (BT 183ff). Nothing would have significance, and there could be neither world nor *Dasein*, in the absence of an understanding rooted in our future-directed projects.

Our everyday Being-in-the-world, then, is 'care': the Being of creatures 'already-in', 'alongside' and 'ahead-of'. Less

jargonistically: our everyday existence is necessarily that of future-directed, purposive agents, absorbedly engaged in dealings
with a significant world into which we have been 'thrown', its
contours of significance — and the possibilities for action that
these offer — already broadly mapped out for us. Three points
about care deserve elaboration. First, the components of care
are mutually interdependent. No one could be 'alongside' things
in the world who was not 'already-in' it and 'ahead-of' himself
— and vice-versa. Thus, we never just have 'moods' or just understand something. 'Situatedness always has its understanding...
Understanding always has its mood' (BT 182). A world is only
'lit up' for someone situated, absorbed and 'projecting' — all
three.

Second, it is hard to exaggerate the degree to which, for
Heidegger, care is 'primordially' both public and unreflective or
'non-thematic'. A 'mood', for example, is not in the first instance a private, 'psychical... inner condition' which then 'puts
its mark on Things and persons' (BT 176). Rather, we are
'thrown' into the shared 'moods' and attitudes of our times, ones
implicit and manifest in the ways people go about things and
respond to circumstances. Similarly, our understanding of the
significations of things — like our grasp of language — is necessarily a shared one, a matter of participating in a public understanding, and is primarily manifested not in conscious judgements
about meanings, but in a smooth, unreflective 'coping' with
things. Meaning, so to speak, is use.

It is at this point that Heidegger's departure from Husserl's
phenomenology is apparent. According to Husserl, our relation
to the world is 'intentional'. To perceive or hope for a particular
thing, I must 'direct' myself towards it — 'intend' it — through
a 'posited meaning' rather as, on one view, I can only refer to
something with a word *via* a prior grasp of that word's meaning.

Just as I only refer to X if X 'satisfies' the meaning of the expression I use, so it is only X that I perceive or hope for if it 'satisfies' the meaning 'posited' as part of my act of perceiving or hoping. Heidegger agrees that we are related to the world 'intentionally', directed towards things through an understanding of significance and meanings, rather than, say, through causal interaction. What he entirely rejects is Husserl's 'perverted' and 'erroneous subjectivizing of intentionality': his treatment of meanings as the products or ingredients of inner mental acts. 'The idea of a subject which has intentional experiences merely inside its own sphere and is not yet outside it... is an absurdity' (BP 64). Intentionality is neither private, inner, nor mental: rather it is 'the character of what we call comporting', one of Heidegger's names for our 'concernful' dealings with things. As such, it is a feature — indeed, *the* feature — implicit in our shared activities. The meanings we recognize in the world about us are not 'posits' of mental acts, but are grasped in and through our engagement with the world.

It was Husserl's 'erroneous subjectivizing' of intentionality that allowed him to perform his disastrous *epoche*, his 'bracketing' of the existence of the real world in order then to focus on our mental acts. After all, just as words, on the view mentioned above, could have meanings without referring to anything in reality so, on Husserl's account, our intentional acts might correspond to nothing 'out there'. For Husserl, therefore, as for Descartes, there arises 'the problem of the external world'. How do I know there is anything outside my own 'inner sphere'? For Heidegger, 'the scandal of philosophy' is not that a proof of the external world has never been given, but that 'such proofs are expected' (BT 249). The problem simply cannot arise, he says, when 'intentionality', our 'mode of access' to the world, is properly understood: for no sense can be made, as we have seen, of

Dasein's existence except in terms of an actual engagement in the world. *Dasein is* its existence in the world, so that to imagine there is no real world is to imagine away ourselves as well. We cannot be 'worldless'.

That said, some of Heidegger's remarks on the issue of 'realism' versus 'idealism' — on the question of things' existence independent of ourselves — are confusing. On the one hand, there is Being only in so far as it is understood by *Dasein* — unsurprisingly if 'Being' refers to the conditions necessary for entities to be encountered by us. On the other hand, these 'entities are, quite independently of the experience by which they are disclosed, the acquaintance in which they are discovered' (BT 228). Strictly, there is no inconsistency here. The conditions for experiencing trees are clearly not independent of us, the experiencers: whereas maybe the trees themselves are. Still, one wonders what this talk of independence amounts to, given Heidegger's insistence that things — trees as much as equipment like hammers —are what they are in virtue of their 'showing up' for us within the 'clearing' formed by our practical engagement in the world, a world itself defined as a totality of significance for us. Heidegger wonders this, too, and returns to the issue in his later writings, as we'll see in Ch. 6.

The third and final remark to make about Heidegger's account of our Being-in-the-world as 'care' may depress those who have struggled to follow it. It has, we are told, only been a 'preparatory analysis of *Dasein*' (BT 274). It is incomplete, first, because it has only been an account of Dasein's 'average everyday' or 'inauthentic' existence, and hence must be rounded out with an account of what it is to exist 'authentically' or 'as-a-whole'. It is incomplete, second, because a full account of Being-in-the-world — indeed, of Being generally — requires an account of time. *Dasein* is essentially temporal in nature, pointing towards the future in which it is 'ahead-of-itself', the present it is 'alongside', and the past which is 'already' there for it. No understanding of this temporal structure is possible, according to Heidegger, without an understanding of time itself. In *Being and Time*, in fact, he has little to say about the nature of time, and elsewhere (e.g. BP Part 2) the more fulsome treatment is barely intelligible. Still, we do need to examine his remarks on *Dasein*'s temporal structure, as well as those on 'authenticity'. Both are interesting in themselves, as well as for their bearing on Heidegger's political adventures.

4. Authenticity, Heritage and Politics

Much of Heidegger's fascination, I suggested, is owed to his blending of large philosophical issues with cultural critique. The account of our Being-in-the-world described in Ch. 3 addressed the former. We now need to consider its relation to Heidegger's evaluation of the modern human condition and the remedies for it which, for a time, he entertained. But we at once run into a problem. Admirers like Hannah Arendt and detractors like Theodor Adorno are agreed that Heidegger's impact upon young people in the 1920s and '30s was largely due to their sense that here, especially in its notion of authenticity, was a philosophy that directly addressed the conduct of their lives in what Heidegger himself called a 'destitute age'. Yet in *Being and Time* he disclaimed any critical intent: in particular, the description of ordinary, inauthentic existence was not to be taken as a 'night view' of *Dasein*, a portrait of the 'corruption of human nature' (BT 224). 'Cultural critique' is an expression Heidegger would have hated being applied to what, on his own estimate, was an exercise in 'pure' philosophy, uncovering the necessary features of human existence as such, not an evaluation of the latest stage in human history.

Heidegger's vocabulary, however, was extraordinarily ill-chosen if his enterprise were simply one of 'analysing' our Being-in-the-world . Our ordinary existence is 'inauthentic', a 'flight from' and 'fall into' the 'tranquillizing' ways of that faceless public Heidegger calls 'the They' (or 'the One' —*Das Man*, an expression concocted from the German pronoun *man*, 'one' as in 'One doesn't do that sort of thing here'). For the most part we are 'under the dictatorship of the They', 'sucked into [its] turbulence', and as such are 'alienated' or 'uprooted' from ourselves. To pretend that no 'night view' of our ordinary condition is intended by such terminology is surely disingenuous. So why does Heidegger disclaim this intent? One reason is his keenness to distance himself from those 'higher journalists', professional *Schwarzseher*, whose understanding of human existence he deemed shallow. A better, if insufficient, reason is to avoid the impression that inauthentic life is a contingent, passing phenomenon, a '"fall" from a purer and higher "primal status"' (BT 220). Far from being our primal condition, authentic existence is only a 'modification' of, and never a total departure from, life 'sunk' in the They. Still, this point, while well-taken, is hardly enough to justify the disclaiming of all critical intent: not, certainly, given Heidegger's insistence that, with 'resoluteness', a person *can* achieve a degree of authenticity and thereby approximate to being what he truly is.

Nor can it be doubted that Heidegger's depiction of inauthentic life is peculiarly appropriate to modernity, to the age of mass society and 'the common man'. The extent of the They's 'dominion' varies in history, he remarks, and it is plain that the dominion he describes is at once very extensive and recent — a description owing much to Kierkegaard's polemics against 'The Public' in a book significantly titled *The Present Age*. In life under the dictatorship of the They, 'averageness' and 'levelling down' prevail. 'We take pleasure as *they* take pleasure... find "shocking" what *they* find shocking'. At the same time, the They imagines that 'one is leading a full and genuine life' and encourages 'uninhibited bustle', 'versatile curiosity and "knowing it all"' which masquerade as genuine understanding. 'In awaiting the next new thing, [the They] has already forgotten the old one', and stale 'truths' are passed along by the 'idle chatter' that has replaced genuine discourse (BT 164f, 222f, 443). Who can doubt that Heidegger was here describing modern, mass-media demotic society? That this was his target was to become apparent by the 1930s, with open references to a recent 'tranformation of men into a mass', a new 'hatred of everything free and creative' (IM 38).

It emerged at the end of the previous chapter that Heidegger's account of Being-in-the-world was, so far, incomplete. It has failed, he says, to portray *Dasein's* 'Being-a-whole', and for two reasons. First, it has described only *in*authentic existence. Second, it has only spoken of *Dasein's* existence '"*between*" birth and death': a 'total' account would have to incorporate these 'limits'. A complete account of Being-in-the-world — of Being-a-whole — would, that is, include depictions of authentic existence and of our relations to birth (or 'heritage') and death. The two components, it turns out, are closely connected, for authenticity requires a proper stance towards one's heritage and death. Put differently, only a person whose life is a 'whole' through integrating its outer 'limits' lives authentically.

Authenticity is introduced immediately after the initial characterization of *Dasein* as something whose Being is an 'issue' for it and which *is* its possibilities. How it exists matters to it and its existence is intelligible only in terms of the possibilities it pursues. But there is one overriding 'choice' it must make which settles or indelibly colours the way in which *Dasein* resolves its 'issue' and fixes on its possibilities. '[I]t *can*... "choose" itself and win itself; it can also lose itself and never win itself; or only "seem" to' (BT 68). Only when it makes the former 'choice, to 'become something of its own', is *Dasein* authentic. The German word is *eigentlich*, whose stem is the word for 'own', as in 'her own room': hence colloquialisms like 'being one's own man' and 'doing one's own thing' give some flavour of Heidegger's notion of authenticity. But only a flavour: to learn more, we need to turn to the 'mood' which, he says, first gives us some intimation of the possiblilty of living authentically and which would inevitably accompany any such life — *Angst* (which I'll generally use in preference to its usual translation, 'anxiety', whose connotations of nail-biting and panic-attacks are best set aside).

An original immersion in the ways of the They is, we saw, necessary: without it, a person would be without any grasp of the possibilities open to him. Inauthentic existence is therefore the 'primordial' condition of which authenticity is a 'modification'. The *degree* to which most people remain under the 'dictatorship' of the They, and so fail to 'modify' their existence, reflects however a 'turning away' or 'flight' from their 'ownmost Being', one motivated by avoidance of *Angst*, an 'uncanny' mood, 'oppressive and stifling', from which people understandably recoil. To serve as a motive for 'flight' from authenticity, *Angst* must also intimate what such an existence might be like. As with other moods, it is also a form of understanding. What, then, does *Angst* intimate?

Unlike ordinary fear, its object is not some 'entity within-the-world', such as a vicious dog. Indeed, during *Angst*, objects lose their importance, everything 'sinks away' into 'utter insignificance'. It is a mood of 'uncanniness', of not being 'at home' in the world. No longer 'absorbed' in the world and getting on with ordinary business, 'everyday familiarity collapses' for the anxious person (BT 232-3). As things within the world 'sink away', it is the world as such and our relation to it which come into focus. In *Angst*, it is appreciated, however dimly, that the world is, so to speak, a product of the They's interpretations, that the possibilities which the They puts on offer are not the only ones, that a different world of significance is open to us to forge. *Angst*, then, 'individualizes' *Dasein*, for it 'makes manifest... its *Being-free* for the freedom of choosing itself', of living authentically (BT 232). Like the youthful hero of some 19th C. *Bildungsroman* who awakes one morning to realize that the boundaries of his parents' parish are not those of the whole universe, so the anxious person experiences a freedom from the world that has hitherto dictated the limits of his understanding and vision. In both cases, the penalty is an unnerving sense of no longer being 'at home', while the reward, for those who do not at once 'turn away' back into the security of 'home', is an 'unshakeable joy' in the prospect of a promised freedom.

If *Angst* in general intimates the possibility of 'modifying' an existence 'sunk' in the They into an 'individualized', authentic one, it is through a particular kind of *Angst*, 'anxiety in the face of *death*', that one's 'ownmost potentiality-for-Being' is most vividly encountered (BT 295). This is not to be confused with the fear of death that occurs when brakes fail or pains shoot through the chest. Indeed, it is not death as a clinical episode which concerns Heidegger: not only because there are other ways, such as severe brain-damage, in which a distinctively human existence can end, but because it is not this end that he has in mind by 'death'. Rather, 'death' is a 'way of Being' or living *towards* one's end. *Angst* in the face of death is *Dasein*'s sense of 'Being *towards* its end' (BT 295). But why should this be described as *Angst*, an 'uncanniness' that 'individualizes'? In part, the point is akin to Dr. Johnson's, that the prospect of death 'concentrates the mind wonderfully'. The They likes to foster the comfortable attitude that death, while inevitable, is always 'a long way off', nothing therefore to 'dwell on'. When, instead, I 'anticipate' it as an ever-present possibility, I take stock of my life and the significance or otherwise of its engagements. In doing so, I am 'liberated' from those which I see as having been 'accidentally thrust' upon me. My 'tenaciousness' to what I now recognize myself to have been just 'thrown' into gets 'shattered' (BT 308).

More crucially, 'anticipation' of my death induces a sense of my 'Being-a-whole', for I am then capable of 'taking the *whole* of [my existence] in advance', viewing the possibilities that lie before me in relation to that final one, my death (BT 309). Lacking such a view, I am in the position of a novelist with no conception of his book's ending, for I am without guidance on structuring my life in a coherent fashion. One possibility, one episode, follows another, but without direction. Once I do range the possibilities ahead of me in anticipation of their coming to an end, I also come to recognize the unique individuality of my life. For while the episodes which belong to it — getting married, becoming a lecturer, and so on — are ones that might figure in anyone else's life, the way in which I gather them into an integrated whole is uniquely mine. This is what Heidegger means when he writes that my death cannot be delegated, that 'no one can take the Other's dying away from him' (BT 284). The point is not that a person cannot die in another's place: think of Sidney Carton taking Charles Darnay's place on the scaffold. It is, rather, that dying in the sense of living in anticipation of death is necessarily an individual path. In its externals, of course, my path might look like those trodden by others: but mine, unlike theirs, incorporates *my* estimate of its significance and direction. True, others can also estimate my life, sum it up as a whole — as an honest, but ultimately self-defeating one, say — but the way in which I respond to their estimates and weave them into my own itself constitutes a significant aspect of my life and is one for which I alone can be responsible.

Heidegger now raises two problems. Granted that *Angst*, especially in the form of anxiety towards death, intimates the theoretical possibility of authentic, individualized existence, is this any more than theoretical? Might it not be 'fantastical' to suppose that *Dasein* could really recover from 'its lostness in the They'? And, second, even if the possibility is a real one, is it one that is genuinely 'demanded' of us? Why should we not regard the attempt to 'be authentic' as a misguided and pathetic one which can only alienate a person from the one thing capable of giving to life some solidity and sense — namely, 'tranquil' immersion in the established ways of one's community? Such, after all, would have been the view in many cultures prior to our more 'individualist' era.

Heidegger answers these questions by introducing the notion of *conscience*. Conscience is experienced as a 'call' or 'voice', and what it calls us to we are bound to regard as both feasible and required of us. In his sense, conscience is not a moral authority — God's, our parents' or society's — which we have internalized and which pricks us when we fail to toe the line. Indeed, it 'gives no information... has nothing to tell' about the things we ought or ought not to do. Rather, 'conscience summons *Dasein*'s Self from its lostness in the They' (BT 318-9), and this deserves to be called 'conscience' since the summons is heard as passing a verdict of 'Guilty!' on us. The point is not that we are guilty because we go around doing despicable things, for *'Dasein as such is guilty'* (BT 331). This, if I understand Heidegger's tortuous discussion of that Kierkegaardian utterance, is because there is no final foundation or justification for the possibilities a person adopts. Our existence has a 'null basis'. This is so whether I live authentically or quiescently following in the footsteps of the They. The difference is that, in the former case, I recognize this 'null basis'. Conscience therefore summons me to '*be* "guilty" *authentically*'. It 'calls *Dasein* forth to the possibility of taking over [its own] existence', in full appreciation of the 'null basis', the lack of foundational reasons, for the decisions it will take (BT 333). The import, then, of that uncanny 'voice' which disturbs our easy absorption in the world of the They is that, as inauthentic, we have abandoned responsibility for — left it to others to decide — what we know, deep down, is something for which we alone, and not 'the order of things', must answer for. It is the 'voice' which intimates that, as Sartre was to put it, we generally live as cowards.

Combining his discussions of *Angst*, 'anticipation' of death and conscience, Heidegger arrives at his final gloss on authenticity: it is 'anticipatory resoluteness'. This is the existence intimated by *Angst* and demanded by the call of conscience: only in anticipatory resoluteness is *Dasein*'s potentiality for its 'ownmost possibility... struck wholly into the conscience' (BT 354). 'Resoluteness' is defined, unappetizingly, as 'reticent self-projection upon one's ownmost Being-guilty, in which one is ready for *Angst*' (BT 343). The 'resolute' person 'reticently' withdraws from the hubbub and 'idle chatter' of the They, holding himself open to hearing and acting upon the summons to 'take over' an 'individualized' responsibility for his life as a whole. 'Resoluteness' does not require that we act in this or that particular way and opt for this rather than that 'ideal of existence'. Even less does it require the making of robust commitments to which one should stick come hell or high water. Instead, it 'calls us forth into the Situation' (BT 347), into a clear and honest appreciation of where we are placed, of what it is that calls for decision, and away, therefore, from the They's facile interpretations which serve only to 'close off' the nature of our Situation. Appreciation of the Situation will not, in itself, prescribe the decisions that should be taken. '*Only* the resolution itself can give the answer' (BT 345).

Moreover, any such decision or resolution must be provisional. The 'steadiness' of resoluteness does not reside in bull-headed determination to stick to one's decision come what may, but in constantly 'hold[ing] oneself free for the possibility of taking it back' (BT 355).

That fundamental 'choice' between authentic and inauthentic existence which Heidegger offers us does not sound an enviable one. It seems to be a choice between a life under the dictatorship of the They and an 'individualized' one in which we are alienated from, no longer 'at home' in, the world of our fellows, and in which, moreover, no guidance is yet offered for how we should act in the face of the Situation that conscience summons us to appreciate. Quiescent abdication from one's own self and anxious solitude seem to exhaust the menu placed before us. Such indeed was the impression that Heidegger's existentialist admirers were content to glean from *Being and Time*. But they didn't read far enough, for towards the end of the book Heidegger proceeds both to soften the contrast between authentic solitude and inauthentic community and to suggest how the authentic agent might be guided towards possibilities on which to resolve.

To understand these developments, we need to recall that other, earlier 'limit' to life — namely *birth*. So far the discussion has focussed on *Dasein*'s 'facing forward', towards death: it is now time to consider what is always 'behind it' as it 'stretches along between birth and death', for otherwise it is not *Dasein*'s Being-a-*whole* which is explicated (BT 425). By 'birth', Heidegger does not mean birth, any more than by 'death' he meant death. As 'death' referred to our our Being-towards-death, so 'birth' refers to our 'Being-towards-the-beginning'. This 'beginning' is what he calls 'heritage', that which has been 'handed down' to us as historically located creatures. This heritage is not to be equated with the conditions into which we are 'thrown', for these constitute our world as structured and articulated by the They, and the They inevitably ignores, distorts or trivializes our heritage. Either the They dismisses the past as old hat and 'seeks the modern', makes it 'unrecognizable', or reduces it to a repository of quaint traditions only to be disinterred on special occasions, like the trooping of the colour. Far from our heritage dictating the shape of everyday, inauthentic existence, it is precisely 'in terms of the heritage... that resoluteness... takes over' that the possibilities of authentic existence are 'disclosed' (BT 435). In properly taking over our heritage, we 'snatch' ourselves back from the 'comfortableness, shirking, and taking things lightly' of the They.

This time, moreover, we are not left without guidance as to the possibilities on which to resolve, for the 'authentically historical' person who 'takes over' his heritage will draw these possibilities precisely *from* that heritage. For what the heritage offers are 'the possibilities of the *Dasein* that has-been-there', the decisions and ways of life adopted by our forebears which are open to us to 'repeat', for example by 'choosing a hero' from the past, and — with due appreciation of the new context — emulate. Indeed, 'revering the repeatable possibilities of existence' is to revere 'the sole authority' which people can pit against the dictatorship of the They and, in so doing, become free (BT 437, 443). Only in the light of a heritage, Heidegger argues, are our horizons widened so that we can enjoy a 'clear vision' of the Situation in which we are placed and hence authentically respond to it. *Dasein*, recall, is essentially temporal in nature. In everyday, 'average' life, it is presently absorbed 'alongside' things in a world it is already 'thrown' into 'for the sake of' realizing its projects in the future. But we are now in a position to define an authentic mode of temporality or historicality: *Dasein*'s being 'in the moment of vision for "its time"', a vision of its Situation which requires both recall of its heritage and 'anticipation' of death (BT 437). The authentic person, then, is one who, determined to make of his life an integrated whole, is able to understand and properly respond to the Situation he is in by bringing to bear upon it the lessons of tradition.

A heritage, of course, is not mine alone, though how I 'take it over' is my doing. The 'fateful destiny' to be gleaned from a heritage is that of a 'community, a people... [a] generation'. To live as an 'authentically historical' person, then, is not to 'soar above' or 'float free' from my fellows, but to 'exist essentially in Being-with-Others' who have also inherited such a destiny. Hence the dichotomy which Heidegger's 'choice' between authentic and inauthentic existence seemed to imply — solipsistic alienation from society *versus* sheepish refuge in the They — turns out to be a false one. By 'taking over' the heritage handed down to me, I at once 'snatch' myself from the comfortable embrace of the They and find a new 'home' in a 'people' or 'generation' which shares that inheritance. Heidegger's authentic person, though 'individualized', is not the existentialist 'loner', necessarily at odds with his society, who stalks the novels of Albert Camus. On the contrary, his 'resoluteness', if it is to have any issue and direction, requires identification with 'a people's destiny', and only then can *Angst* be transformed from a state of 'uncanniness' into one of 'unshakeable', if 'sober', joy at recovery from 'lostness in the They'.

To see how Heidegger thought that a heritage might be 'taken over', a 'moment of vision' seized, and the Situation authentically responded to, we must turn to the writings and speeches during his Freiburg Rectorate in 1933-4. Certainly these were packed with what Adorno called 'the jargon of authenticity' — 'resoluteness', 'destiny', 'will': as indeed were those of a man born in the same year as Heidegger — Adolf Hitler. A huge literature has mushroomed on the connection between the philosophy of *Being and Time* and Heidegger's perception, never disowned, of the 'greatness and glory of [a] new dawn' with Hitler's coming to power. At one extreme is the view that there is no logical connection at all; at the other, claims that Nazism is 'latent in' or 'absolutely coherent with' his philosophy — one which, though modified since 1928, was not yet at least an abandonment of the earlier position.

Those who take the former view see in the writings of 1933-4 an 'obscene recolouring', as Jürgen Habermas calls it, of 'the jargon of authenticity', a perverse recasting of claims about individual authenticity into ones about the collective destiny of a *Volk* or nation. Certainly one finds lines which might have come from *Being and Time* except that collective terms have replaced the word '*Dasein*'. Thus, 'the will to self-responsibility' is now something credited to whole nations, and it is 'the entire people' who, collectively, must make the momentous choice 'whether it wants its own existence [or] does *not* want it' (HC 52, 47). But it is mistaken to accuse Heidegger of disingenuously dragooning 'the jargon of authenticity' into the service of a new political creed. For we saw above that individual authenticity is impossible except as a member of a 'people... a generation' which 'takes over' its heritage. The shift from individual to collective had already occurred in *Being and Time*.

That said, nothing in the earlier work prepares one for the degree to which Rector Heidegger is happy to see the individual swallowed into the collective. Consider, for example, his account of freedom. He had never equated this with 'mere absence of constraint' by others. Rather, freedom was 'engagement in the disclosure of beings as such' (BW 128). Whatever that meant, it hardly seemed to endorse his 1933 declamation to students and colleagues that, with so-called 'academic freedom' banished, they

Everett Library
Queens College

will now find true freedom in 'forms of service' to the State and 'placing themselves under the law of their essence' (HC 34-5).

This suggests that the second view — that a predilection for Nazism is virtually entailed by Heidegger's philosophy — is also exaggerated. Even when softened into the claim that there is considerable consonance between the two, the reason given by some commentators is unpersuasive. For them, the link is the mixture of nihilism and 'decisionism' to be found both in *Being and Time* and in the political manifestos. Does Heidegger not, in the former, urge 'doing violence' to all prevailing norms of understanding and advocate a resolute decisiveness in courses of action that are without any further justification? And is this not the language of Nazism, fully apparent in the Rector's own exhortation to 'German men and women' to free themselves from 'the idol of thought' and instead 'be resolved to action' (HC 51)? But it distorts Heidegger's position, both in 1928 and 1933, to foist on him a doctrine of 'action for action's sake', for this ignores, once again, the crucial role of heritage. We may indeed 'do violence' to the They's understanding of our Situation, but only whilst 'reverently preserving the existence that has-been-there' (BT 448) and taking this as our guide to decisions. In 1936 a former pupil of Heidegger reports meeting his old teacher in Rome and being told that 'his concept of "historicity" was the basis of his political "engagement"' (HC 142). Rightly or wrongly, Heidegger perceived in Hitler — who liked being painted wearing a medieval suit of armour — someone with a real sense of his nation's historical destiny, someone who had, as Heidegger advocated, 'chosen' past heroes to emulate.

In pointing this out, one is agreeing that there is, after all, consonance between Heidegger's philosophy and his political stance. Nor does it end here, for at the very least the philosophy suggests a sympathy for the *style* of politics engaged in by fascists (though not by them alone). This is politics in the apocalyptic style: politics as the arena where big, radical decisions are called for in a struggle against the forces responsible for a crisis of civilization — decisions that can only be made by the few men, or single man, with an insight into the caesura, the moment of destiny, that has been reached, and with the will and power to carry it through. The apocalyptic tone may be muted in *Being and Time*, though surrounding writings make it clear that, even then, Heidegger was sympathetic to the 'reactionary modernist' sense of a Europe in decline and crisis under the dictatorship of the They, a crisis to be faced with something more radical than nostalgic yearnings for a past order. By the 1930s Heidegger is explicit that 'the spiritual decline of the earth is... far advanced' and the situation of Europe 'catastrophic'. If Europe is not to suffer 'annihilation', then a 'great decision' must be made 'in terms of new spiritual energies unfolding historically from out of the centre' (IM 38ff). That centre is Germany, and at the centre of Germany is Hitler.

It is no surprise, therefore, to find Heidegger excoriating liberal democracy, especially in the United States, as a 'moribund pseudocivilization', in which people are levelled down to a mere 'mass', where creative spirit is 'hated', and where a boxer can get regarded as 'a nation's great man'. But democracy was not the only alternative to fascism on offer. What about Soviet communism? This is no better, for 'Russia and America are metaphysically the same', equally 'levelling', equally guilty of 'enfeeblement of the spirit' (IM 38, 45). But why should this be? After all, communism is also politics in the apocalyptic style, premised on a vision of an historical process which has now reached a revolutionary stage calling for the decisive leadership of a vanguard with the will to see the revolution through.

Herbert Marcuse judged that, while Heidegger's philosophy

was favourable to totalitarian politics, it was not intrinsically *fascist:* a view reiterated by one recent commentator when he writes that it was 'only a mix of opportunism and personal preference,... not anything built into his fundamental ontology', which explains Heidegger's plumping for Nazism over Bolshevism (Guignon, in Dreyfus & Hall [eds.] 142). But while pragmatism and personality may have played their role, there were deeper reasons why Bolshevism could not have been Heidegger's choice. The first derives from the critique of technology which he was beginning to develop. Russia was as bad as America in being infected with a 'dreary technological frenzy' threatening 'the destruction of the earth, the standardization of man' (IM 45). It was Heidegger's belief, shared by many Nazi voters and affirmed in many of Hitler's speeches, that the Führer was the champion of country life, that he appreciated the damage wrought by industrial urbanization on Germans who would, therefore, 'be returned to the soil'. The reasons for Heidegger's opposition to technology will emerge in Ch. 5, but they are certainly more 'fundamental' than any 'personal preference' reflecting his own bucolic roots. One deserves to be mentioned here. In a 1934 radio talk, Heidegger said, in romantic vein, that 'philosophical work' belongs less in the academic's study than 'right here in the midst of the peasant's work... It is intimately rooted in... the life of the peasants' (in Zimmermann 71). Operating here, presumably, is the idea that the peasant, like the traditional craftsman, is the possessor of that 'primordial' practical understanding 'in the hands' which the rest of us, seduced by the 'theoretical', have largely lost. In that respect, the peasant is closer to Being — to what makes any understanding possible in the first place — than the city-slicker or the scientist.

A second and related 'fundamental' reason for Heidegger's opting for Nazism over Bolshevism was the better prospects for the universities, and within them for philosophy in particular, under the former. It needs to be stressed that he saw his own role as that of introducing the *Führerprinzip* into the universities so as to reverse a perceived decay of university learning. This decay was due, first, to 'the encapsulation of knowledge into separate disciplines', no longer under the sovereign guidance of philosophy. 'All science is philosophy .. whether it wills it or not' (HC 31ff). Science is only possible and made 'secure' on the basis of 'fundamental ontology' which, among its other accomplishments, uncovers the conditions of scientific knowledge. The decay was due, second, to an increasingly pragmatic, instrumentalist self-image of the particular sciences as so many 'serviceable tools' in the technological enterprise. On both counts, no redress could be expected from Bolshevism. Despite his respect for Marx, Heidegger regarded Marxism as a social science, not a philosophy in his sense, and unfitted therefore to serve as the unifying basis of the sciences which it had become in Russia. Moreover, Marxism was the very paradigm of an instrumentalist conception of the sciences, intent on gearing 'the use of intelligence... to the regulation and domination of the material conditions of production' (IM 47).

Hitler, on the other hand, was as Heidegger saw it on the side of philosophy. Was he not the leader of that 'most metaphysical nation', Germany, and the sender of such encouraging telegrams as 'May the strength of German philosophy contribute to the foundation of the German ideology!'? Hitler would surely be more favourable than Stalin to the 'self-assertion' of the university under the banner of philosophy, the most 'essential' enquiry. It is not strained to compare Heidegger's attitude with that of Plato in the *Republic*: for there, as in the Germany Heidegger anticipated, it is not only that the greatest servants of the State are philosophers, but the State owes much of its glory to being a fit place for philosophy to flourish within.

For Heidegger, one of his students remarked, Hitler was not only on the side of philosophy but 'on the side of Being'. What this means can only be properly illuminated after we have looked, in Ch. 5, at 'the history of Being' which Heidegger was soon to start telling. Suffice it to say here that he was already beginning to talk about Being in a more 'mystical' tone than in *Being and Time*. The ancients' 'beginning' of the disclosure of Being is now seen as part of the heritage which we need to 'repeat' and which will enable that 'moment of vision' into our 'catastrophic' situation: but this is an exercise attended with 'strangeness, darkness, insecurity' (IM 39). It is not at all the kind of exercise engaged in by the mere social historians and social scientists of Marxism, but one to be entrusted to a 'hero' with a quite different and mysterious insight — under the guidance, doubtless, of the sage that Heidegger hoped to be recognized as in his, that most metaphysical, nation.

5. Technology and 'The History of Being'

Whatever hopes Heidegger initially invested in Hitler, disillusion with National Socialism became increasingly apparent in his lectures after 1936, prudently oblique though his criticisms generally were. We find, for example, sardonic references to a craze for uniforms and mass-meetings and to 'peddlars' of 'biologistic' ideology. Three aspects of this disillusion deserve special mention. First, it was becoming clear to Heidegger that Nazism lacked the capacity adequately to respond to 'the encounter between global technology and modern man' — the very capacity in which he had once glimpsed 'the inner truth and greatness of this movement' (IM 199). The Nazis, he later judged, 'moved in th[e] direction' of such a response more than the Russians and Americans, but were 'far too limited in their thinking' properly to fathom the nature of modern technology and hence to cope with it (HC 111). Nazism, therefore, could offer no panacea for man's 'homelessness', now seen as the product of that 'global conquest of the earth' by technology in which Nazism, too, was implicated (Ne 248).

Second, Heidegger now rejected the ideal of an authentic *Volk* in which he had earlier discerned the antidote both to stagnant conformism and to rootless individualism. Far from collectivism being a counter to the 'subjectivism' responsible for selfish individualism, it is merely subjectivism writ large. Positing the *Volk* as 'the goal and purpose' is a hubristic continuation of '"liberal", "ego-centred" thinking' (GA 65/319). In both cases, man is being set up as the centre and measure of his universe. Finally, Heidegger has now lost confidence in 'heroes' of the 'resolute' iron-man type — Hitler, for example — to decide the course of history by seizing on a people's 'heritage'. Possibly Heidegger's own failure to put the *Führerprinzip* into effect at Freiburg influenced his thinking here. Be that as it may, it is now his view that even 'leaders' are virtual puppets on the world-stage. So-called 'men of will' are more willed than willing, and only 'appear to enact', caught up as they are in an 'anarchy of catastrophes'. At best they possess an 'instinct' which equips them to be 'directive organs' of an impersonal 'mobilization' in whose 'service' they are (HC 81ff).

These three elements in Heidegger's reappraisal of Nazism are closely related. Technology, increasingly perceived as 'the most monstrous transformation our planet has ever undergone' (EG 17), is the final product of that subjectivism — or 'anthropocentrism' or 'humanism' — which, in the modern era, takes the form of 'the will to power', a relentless attempt, individual or collective, to subjugate the earth out of economic motives. Yet it is an attempt over which no one, not even a 'leader', has real control: rather, as in a 'totally mobilized' war with a momentum of its own, individuals and nations become 'resources', 'human materials', consumed in an inexorable process. There is a deeper respect, however, in which the three elements are related. Technology, subjectivism, and the submission of people to forces they do not control are all themes in what Heidegger calls his 'history of Being'. Technology, we are told, is 'a destiny within the history of Being', its latest and perhaps most enduring phase, and one which, in the shape of national economic self-aggrandizement, 'completes' a longer-standing tendency towards 'subjectivity's unconditioned self-assertion'

(BW 220f). This history of Being, morever, though it 'needs and uses' human beings, is not of human making.

Readers will rightly wonder if 'disillusion' is the most apt word for Heidegger's attitude after 1936. It is not so much, it seems, that the Nazis failed in what he thought they could and should achieve as that he has altered his view of what this is. At the very least, a new understanding of technology and subjectivity seems to have crept in. But more than that, the very talk of a history of Being appears to mark a major shift in his wider philosophy. After all, Being as we characterized it when discussing *Being and Time* — the conditions necessary for anything to be experienced or understood (see p. 23) — was not something that could sensibly be said to *have a history*. Nor would it have made sense to speak of Being, so characterized, as a 'power' which 'comes to destiny' by 'giving itself' and, in the process, 'sends' or 'throws' man into his existence — which is precisely how Heidegger does now speak (BW 215ff).

Clearly there has been a 'turn' (*Kehre*) in Heidegger's thinking. When this occurred exactly, and wherein it consists, is a matter for debate among commentators, one scarcely clarified by Heidegger's own comments on the 'endless babble' about this 'turn'. His usual line was that commentators misunderstood the central theses of *Being and Time*, which were perfectly consonant with his later thought. This is hard to swallow, for although earlier themes recur, they do so in a strange and remote key. For example, 'homelessness', experienced in *Angst*, was described in the earlier work, as a condition of human beings *as such*, an essential aspect of their existence. But by 1946, homelessness has become a historical phenomenon, a 'symptom' of the technological age's 'oblivion of Being'.

I postpone until Ch. 6 a fuller attempt to understand this 'turn' and the revised conceptions of Being, truth and human existence which are involved, for these are best approached after sketching the main episodes in the history of Being, especially its latest one, technology. Still, something needs to be said in advance for any appreciation of what Heidegger is trying to do.The shift of key comes with the insistence in the later writings that 'the existence of man is historical as such' (BW 216). In *Being and Time*, of course, Heidegger stressed that human beings are historical in the sense of being born into an 'already' interpreted world and a 'heritage' for them to take over. But aside from a rather casual mention of 'primitive' people (BT 81f), no allowance was made for the possibility that human beings might differ over time in those basic structures of experience and understanding which the book aimed to identify. Experiencing things in the first instance as ready-to-hand equipment was, for example, held to be a necessary — and therefore unchanging — aspect of *Dasein*. It is this ahistorical conception of human existence and hence of the 'world' which human beings are 'in' which Heidegger abandons.

With this abandoned, our understanding of Being must alter. It can no longer be identified with *the* conditions for anything to be encountered, for there aren't any — only a succession of different conditions under which things are variously experienced. If we are still to characterize Being as 'that on the basis of which entities are understood' and experienced, as a 'source' of their being 'present' to us, then it is crucial to recognize that it is must therefore be the 'source' of the historically shifting conditions which make such understanding and experience possible. Not only must entities 'stand in the open' for us to experience, but 'the path or relation' to them — the conditions presupposed by any given way of experiencing them — must also have been made open (BQ 174). 'Being' now becomes one of Heidegger's names for that which 'gives' these conditions, which 'opens' any particular 'path' to encountering things (as equipment, say, or as holy). Being, he writes, is what determines our experience of things at any given time by 'open[ing] up a region for making entities intelligible' (N 481).

A further point needs to be grasped before we can understand Heidegger's history of Being. Philosophers, we learned in *Being and Time*, have been guilty of insufficiently probing the conditions of experience: they have taken beings for granted, failing to explore the Being on the basis of which they *are* at all. Even less have they paid attention to the mysterious 'source' of these conditions. They have not 'thought Being' in Heidegger's revised sense of this term. Hence philosophy, at least since its earliest times, has involved an 'oblivion of Being', a forgetting of 'the truth of Being'. To this long period of philosophy, Heidegger gives the name 'metaphysics', henceforth a pejorative term in his lexicon. He stresses, however, that metaphysicians have not simply been dolts and that talk of their 'guilt' or 'failure' is misleading. This is because it was inevitable that philosophers — with the exception of a few 'uncanny ones', like the poet Hölderlin and, presumably, himself — should have 'forgotten Being'.

Philosophy was born with the Greeks' 'wonder' at the world and the consequent attempt to investigate all beings, themselves included. In doing so, philosophers were bound to ignore that which made it possible for there to be any beings to investigate and wonder at. This recalls Heidegger's earlier point (see p. 22) that we are generally too absorbed in the things we are 'alongside' to reflect on the conditions necessary for encountering them. 'If we stand in a clearing... we see only what can be found within it... the trees — and precisely not the luminosity of the clearing itself' (BQ 178). The Greeks and their metaphysical successors could not, so to speak, see the light for the trees. That it has not been some mere oversight to ignore 'the truth of

Being' is at least part of what Heidegger means when he speaks of Being as 'self-concealing', 'withdrawing' or 'keeping to itself', and when he refers to the history of philosophy as that of a 'default' on the part of Being itself (Ne 238ff).

The history of Being sounds like a project in comparison with which H.G. Wells' history of the mere world was only moderately ambitious. But what we primarily find in Heidegger's many recountings of his history are accounts of earlier philosophers' *theories* of Being. Is he, then, simply writing a history of philosophy under a pretentious title? No, for his discussion often ranges beyond the confines of professional philosophy and covers, for example, the attitudes implicit in the Roman *imperium*, mediaeval faith in salvation, and above all the driving spirit behind modern technology. More important, perhaps, he insists that philosophers only articulate prevailing ways of experiencing the natural world, human life or whatever: ways which shape or 'gather' a whole culture, its art and politics as much as its theoretical products.

So is Heidegger recounting the epochs of Western history in general, informed perhaps by the conviction that it is 'ideas' which drive that history? No, for in the first place this would imply that human beings are more or less in control of their history, when in fact the successive ways in which things are 'revealed' to people, and hence the intellectual articulations of their experience, are 'destined' by Being. Thinkers and everyone else are 'claimed for history by Being' (N 484). Second, Heidegger's 'epochs' do not correspond to those of orthodox historians. In fact, he is punning when he speaks of epochs, trading on the meaning of the Greek word *epoche*, 'withdrawal'. An epoch of history is a distinctive episode in 'the withdrawal of Being' — a way in which Being is 'forgotten'. Heidegger's history, in effect, is less one of what people have thought and done as of what they have ignored or forgotten.

What, before we turn to his history, is Heidegger's purpose in telling it? He described it as 'eschatological' and might have called it 'soteriological' as well. Not only does the history of Being — of 'the oblivion of Being', metaphysics, that is — have a direction towards an 'end', but that 'end' is something 'monstrous' in the face of which we must nurture the prospect of a 'saving power'. This 'end' is technology, 'the desolation of the earth stemming from metaphysics' (HC 68). Unless we recognize it as the culmination of the metaphysical tradition, we shall neither understand technology nor, therefore, be in a position to prepare for salvation. For this purpose it is crucial, too, to recall the beginning of philosophical tradition. While we cannot repeat the early Greek experience of the world, there was a truth to that experience which has become increasingly obscured and which we must endeavour to recollect. That 'first beginning' by the Greeks may not quite have been Eden, but unless we appreciate the pre-lapsarian truth it contained, we shall be incapable of that 'other beginning [which] experiences the truth of Being' (GA 65/179).

Let's now open Heidegger's history. Although they failed properly to *think* it, the early Greeks — the pre-Socratic philosophers, poets and tragedians — *experienced* Being in an authentic way, as *physis*, a 'self-blossoming emergence' of things, a 'process of arising, of emerging from the hidden' (IM 14-15). This experience of Being was inseparable from a certain understanding of truth and the place of human beings. As the Greek word for truth, *aletheia* ('unveiledness'), suggests, they understood truth as 'the unconcealedness of beings': a being is 'true' when it emerges as it is, unconcealed. The task of man, concomitantly, is to 'guard the truth', to remove the obstacles in the way of things emerging unconcealed, so that they 'might appear... as the beings they are' (BW 210). Human beings are 'called' precisely to serve as the 'clearing' in which things may emerge unveiled.

As we saw, however, once the Greeks, inspired by their 'wonder' at the world about them, began to investigate, it was not the process of emergence, Being, which they investigated, but the things which had emerged, beings. This, the 'decisive moment' in history, the true beginning of metaphysics, occurs with Plato, and therewith 'the great philosophy of the Greeks comes to an end' (BQ 120). Though Plato, Aristotle and their successors will talk of 'Being', this is not Being as originally experienced: rather, it is 'beingness' — the general properties or causes of beings. Thus, true Being for Plato is the world of the Forms or Ideas: a Form being at once what things of a particular kind have in common and the blueprint on the basis of which they are produced by the divine 'Craftsman'. When Plato experiences things in the world as 'appearance', this is no longer 'self-blossoming emergence', but the pale copying by an actual horse or flower of its 'supersensible', prototypical Form.

At this decisive moment, then, the crucial difference between Being and beings is forgotten: Being, no longer appreciated as the ineffable source of beings, becomes something to arrive at by abstraction or inference from beings. It becomes just one more kind of being, however elevated. At best, it becomes the conditions necessary for us to perceive or otherwise encounter things, not the source of those very conditions. When that source, Being, 'discharges itself into beingness', it 'withdraws into concealedness' (N 486). The notions of truth and human being undergo concomitant shifts with this 'discharge'. Truth is no longer grasped as the coming into unconcealment of things: instead, Plato understands it as getting a right view of the Forms. The task of human beings is no longer to 'guard' things in their unconcealedness but to develop the intellectual prowess adequately to grasp their 'essence'. Both changes are apparent in Aristotle: the conception of truth as *aletheia* has 'passed on to a determination of truth as the correctness of an assertion' (BQ 98), and man is defined as *animal rationale*, one creature among others, distinguished only by a capacity to exercise reason in getting assertions right.

Decisive as the Platonic turn was, not all vestiges of the early Greek experience have yet been erased. For example, Aristotle retains something of the vision of Being as *physis*, for his 'substance' is that whereby a thing realizes its *telos*, becoming in actuality what it was potentially. Further progress towards oblivion, however, is made by that 'Platonism for the people' as Heidegger, following Nietzsche, calls Christianity. Being as a source is equated with one special being, God, while the Being of everything else 'consists in its being created by God' (Ne 88). The world is no longer 'self-emerging', but the finished product of a creator. *Physis* has become 'Nature'. Truth is no longer established by insight into the Forms, but through revelation as promulgated in church doctrine. With the rise of Protestantism, morever, the criterion of truth takes a more subjective turn, inner certainty in the form of faith. Such certainty assures us, for instance, of our future salvation. Protestantism also effects an important change in Christians' conception of the proper role of human beings, from that of contemplative submission in God's order to that of 'creativity, previously the unique property of the biblical God', but now a human activity in emulation of Him. Echoing Max Weber's diagnosis of the rise of capitalism under Protestantism, Heidegger writes 'human creativity finally passes over into business enterprise' (QCT 64).

There is still some distance to travel, though, to modern technology's complete oblivion of Being and naked aggression towards the world. Even with Protestantism the inner certainty of faith is not self-guaranteeing: it is answerable to an order that is God's, not man's. Nor can man's creative activity, even 'business enterprise', be wholly unbooted if it is really to emulate God's creativity and respect the world He made for us. In the creator-God, therefore, there is something which, however dimly, recalls the early Greek experience of Being as the mysterious source of beings and of man's role as their guardian. All this changes, however, with the erosion of religious faith and the rise of science, when the place abdicated by God is filled by man himself. We are now in the Cartesian epoch, chronicled in *Being and Time*, when reality is construed as so many objects standing over against subjects, whose mission is accurately to represent these objects, primarily through the methods of mathematical physics.

In the Cartesian epoch, 'beingness is now objectivity'. This may seem an odd way to characterize an epoch which, Heidegger insists, marks a decisive step towards a *subjectivist* view of Being. But, to begin with, that objectivity was only intelligible in relation to subjects, as that which 'stand[s] over against guaranteeing, calculating representation' (HC 70). No subjects, then no objects in the pertinent sense. There is more to it than that, however. Inherited from Christianity was a craving for certainty and this was taken to be, in the first instance, self-certainty, knowledge of the *cogito* and its contents, such as its 'clear and distinct' ideas of motion and extension. Thus a conception of the 'external', 'objective' world was only acceptable if couched in terms of ideas which passed the muster of self-examination. This meant that scientists, whatever they may have thought they were doing, were proceeding on the basis of a 'ground plan of the object-sphere' laid down in advance. Their 'objective' world, far from existing independently of any human conception, was in effect a 'picture', something 'set up by man', the 'representer' (QCT

121, 130). The frank admission of this came with Kant, for whom the necessary structures of the empirical world are those imposed, *a priori*, by the human mind.

But it was Kant, too, with his distinction between the empirical world and the unknowable one of 'things in themselves', who burst the bubble of objective certainty. How can we know that our 'picture', necessary as it may be *for us*, is a true one? The answer to this question, prepared by Hegel but completed by Nietzsche, marks the final phase of metaphysics, that of 'the absolute subjectivity of the will to power'. That question presupposed a distinction between what we hold to be true and what may in fact be true: the solution is to erase that distinction. How the world is, at least in its broad contours, is now simply what we have decided or willed. The terms and concepts in which we describe it are merely those we have constructed as most conducive to obtaining control over the world and our lives, as yielding maximum self-assurance of our capacity to will. The will is 'the sole criterion that guarantees everything', the producer of 'the only order', against which there is nothing else to appeal to (HC 80-1). Being is nothing other than will. With this metaphysics, Platonism is at once reversed and completed. Reversed, since it is the sensuous and animal — 'drives and affects' — which have replaced the 'supersensible' and rational, the Forms, as the nature of Being. Completed, since the departure from the early Greek experience which Plato set in motion is now total. Being as a mysterious source that 'calls' to man whose task is to 'protect' it is now entirely withdrawn and denied. What is, is what we make. If 'nihilism' is denial of Being, then with Nietzsche, despite his claim to 'overcome' the nihilism ensuing from 'the death of God', we have 'nihilism proper', the stark admission of what was always implicit in metaphysics as such.

Before Nietzsche's doctrine of the will to power could be

converted into the technologism of the 20th Century, one more step was required. A 'misled Wagnerian cult' had induced Nietzsche and his followers romantically to locate the proper exercise of this will in the aesthetic 'life-enthusiasm' of the *Übermensch*. Cooler heads were soon to realize, however, that it was in 'the unconditional rule of calculating reason', not 'an opaque chaos of "life"', that the will to power finds fullest expression (HC 75). With this realization, technology has arrived.

Heidegger's critique of technology has been enthusiastically received by many 'eco-philosophers' and environmentalists. This is understandable even if few of them appreciate the place that technology has in Heidegger's historical scheme as the final 'abandonment of Being', and even if his critique appeals to few of the concepts — 'sustainable development', 'intrinsic values in nature', and so on — that today's environmentalists, 'shallow' or 'deep', typically deploy when complaining of modern technology.

By 'technology' Heidegger does not mean technology. For a start, he uses the term in a much wider way than normal, to include 'objectified nature, the business of culture, manufactured politics, and the gloss of ideals overlying everything' (HC 74). More peculiarly, he tells us that technology is 'completely new' and is not, in essence, a matter of 'human doing' or activity at all. 'Technology', it emerges, refers to 'a way of revealing' or 'rendering things manifest' quite different from any previous way, and one that governs the whole of modern life, including politics and 'the business of culture' (QCT 5, 12). It is not a 'human doing', partly because it is not, strictly speaking, a 'doing' at all, and partly because, like other 'ways of revealing', it is 'destined' in the history of Being and not, therefore, something concocted by man.

As a way of revealing, technology is akin to the *techne* of the early Greeks. But whereas the Greek craftsman saw himself as 'bringing forth' the intrinsic properties of the materials, like silver, with which he worked, today's technologist '*challenges* forth' these materials, 'sets upon' them and imposes a 'use-value' on them. Thus 'the earth now reveals itself as a coal mining district, the soil as a mineral deposit', and the Rhine as a 'water power supplier', except when put on call 'for inspection... by the vacation industry'. People no longer honour and cooperate with the earth: rather everything is put on 'standing-reserve', as so much equipment to order, tap and use. To this setting-upon, challenging, ordering way of revealing the world, Heidegger gives the name 'enframing' (*Gestell*). Enframing, therefore, is 'the essence of modern technology' (QCT 14ff). (The technological way of encountering things, it won't have escaped the reader, is close to that experiencing of things as ready-to-hand which, in *Being and Time*, Heidegger took to be the necessarily 'primordial' mode of encounter). Enframing is both continuous with and distinct from the 'objectivity' of the Cartesian epoch. Now, as then, anything that can be encountered is first filtered through a 'ground plan' laid down in advance. But with the emergence of the priority of the will, this 'ground plan' has become an instrumentalist one. Things are what they are in virtue of the use to which they can be put for human purposes. That is why scientific truth has become 'equated with the efficiency of the... effects' which applied science produces (TB 58), and why scientists nowadays are 'miserable slaves' to the hegemony of technology (BQ 6).

What is it that Heidegger finds so 'monstrous' about the technological way of revealing, one that has turned the world into an 'unworld'? First, there is the irony that while technology is the logical outcome of man's desire for self-assurance, for submitting everything to himself, it has come to dominate him. It is not simply, as Spengler grimly predicted, that technology would produce results that no one could control, though that is indeed bound to happen given that it 'drives the earth beyond the... sphere of its possibility' (HC 89). More crucially, human beings become helplessly caught up in the 'total mobilization' that technology requires if it is to press ahead. As Ernst Jünger, the inventor of that phrase and a writer much admired by Heidegger, put it, technology places its 'stamp' upon everything, including people. At the same time, says Heidegger, that he 'exalts himself to the posture of lord of the earth', man himself is 'taken as standing-reserve', as a resource esteemed only for his potential contribution to the technological process (QCT 27). With some prescience, he was warning, in the 1950s, of biotechnology's capacity one day to launch an 'attack... upon the... nature of man compared with which the explosion of the hydrogen bomb means little' (DT 52).

Second, technology produces extreme aimlessness and homelessness. Admittedly, there is the overarching aim of 'maximum yield at the minimum expense', but nothing guides our sense of what should be yielded and why, nor of what to do with it when we have got it. Precisely because 'man stumbles aimlessly about', he is also homeless. At an obvious level, this is due to the destruction of locations, traditions and old certainties, which technology brings in its wake. People become quite literally homeless, as when Germans are 'driven from their native soil [and] resettled in the wastelands of industrial districts' (DT 48), and hardly less literally so when the hydroelectric plant replaces the old bridge across the Rhine that once joined people into a single community. But, at a deeper level, homelessness is 'coming to be the destiny of the world' for all of us, however 'covered up' it is by today's frenetic activity. This is no longer the homelessness of the *Angst*-ridden individual of *Being and Time*, in self-exile from the They, but the 'symptom of oblivion of Being'

(BW 218f). This means at least that technology generates a 'fussing about beings' at the expense of any reflection on the 'source' responsible for the conditions of their being encountered at all. This is homelessness, since it is precisely this 'source' which, in the deepest sense, is man's home — that from which his sustenance and conception of himself are drawn, and to which he has a protective responsibility.

There is another aspect to technology's 'oblivion of Being' which invites Heidegger's final criticism. Technology, he writes, 'drives out every other possibility of revealing' (QCT 27). In previous epochs, a prevailing way of revealing things could not entirely exclude other ways of experiencing them. Technology is different: every potentially rival way of revealing gets sucked into it. For example, the experience of art becomes technologized — not because we have no interest in paintings except for their market value, but because they too are on 'standing-reserve', as things to produce a 'yield' in the form of exciting sensations or relaxation from the pressures of the workplace. This means, for a start, that everything in modern life gets 'levelled' and made 'monotonous'. In part, this is due to technological ingenuity: distance, for example, is erased by TV programmes which bring events in Australia or on the moon into the living-room at the press of a button — a living-room morever which, with its central heating and air-conditioning, immunizes its inhabitants against the differences between the seasons. ('It's wonderful', recently exclaimed the owner of a *de luxe* home in the Californian desert, 'you'd never know you were in the desert!'). More disturbingly, the values and standards by which people live become homogenized across the globe, all of them derived from the imperatives of technology. And if anyone protests, his doing so is then 'explained away' by sociologists or psychologists: his standards merely register a self-serving 'ideology' or 'subjective' feelings not to be taken seriously, therefore, by 'practical' people.

So effectively does technology drive out other possibilities of revealing that its most 'fundamental characteristic' — namely that it *is* a way of revealing — is itself overlooked. Experiencing things instrumentally becomes so entrenched that the very possibility of 'letting beings be' in any other way is excluded from the modern imagination. Herein resides 'the supreme danger', the total 'oblivion of Being' (QCT 26f). Not only is every other way of revealing excluded, so is any sense of what it might be to experience things differently, for any perception that the present way is *a* way has gone. With this, we are at a maximum distance from the early Greeks' conception of Being as *physis*, from their holding themselves open to the 'emergence' of things in all their potential fullness and variety.

What can be done about this 'monstrous' situation? We surely cannot 'push on blindly with technology', but it would be fruitless 'to rebel helplessly... and curse it as the work of the devil'. In his main essay on technology, Heidegger gives us little comfort beyond quoting Hölderlin's conviction that 'where danger is, grows the saving power also' and telling us that we might 'foster' this saving power 'here and now and in humble things' (QCT 25f, 33f). But he also hints that it is in art and poetry, which the Greek concept of *techne* embraced, that the advent of this power might be prepared for. So let us turn to his account of these and to the themes inspired by them which preoccupied Heidegger after 1945.

6. Art, Language, Thinking and Dwelling

It is sometimes suggested that Heidegger turned to art and poetry as remedies for a 'destitute age' out of disillusion with nationalist politics. But of his earliest writings on these topics in the mid-1930s, it would be truer to say that the intention was to refine that politics. Heidegger himself describes these writings as political 'in the most authentic sense' and, for a time, his unbounded enthusiasm for Hölderlin was partly due to a conviction that here was 'the poet of the Germans', whose verses might serve to 'found' and unite the *Volk*.

Even in these writings, there was a further motive for discussing art and poetry: to provide an account, lacking in *Being and Time*, of the status of art-works. They belong, it seems, to none of the categories on offer in that book. A painting, say, does not have the kind of existence people have, *Dasein*. Nor, surely, is it a merely ready-to-hand item of equipment, even if nowadays it is likely to be caught up in the 'art business', as an investment or status symbol with 'use-value'. Nor, finally, is it simply a present-at-hand object to come across and perceive. Modern aesthetics, to be sure, 'turns the art work into an object for our feelings', something to stare at in order to obtain 'art experiences': but then aesthetics is in thrall to the metaphysical tendency to consider everything as an object producing experiences in us subjects (WL 42f). How, then, can art-works be accommodated within the framework of *Being and Time*? The answer is that they cannot be fully accommodated, which is why Heidegger's 'turn' from that book is linked to his reflections on art and poetry. At first he aims only to expand that framework and to slot art-works in as an extra category. Gradually, however, those reflections will induce an overhaul of the framework, a (tacit) confession that, with the preeminence there granted to practical dealings with equipment, it all too faithfully adhered to technological metaphysics. That is why, by 1953, Heidegger can locate in reflections on art and poetry a power to 'save' us from technology.

But let's first go back nearly twenty years. There we find Heidegger distinguishing art-works, 'great' ones at least, from other entities by ascribing three functions to them. First, 'the art-work opens up in its own way the Being of beings', allowing them to show up as the beings they really are. Art, therefore, 'unveils' and hence is 'truth setting itself to work' (BW 166). The point is beautifully illustrated by Heidegger's discussion of Van Gogh's painting of a peasant woman's shoes in which the 'equipmental quality' of shoes is revealed. Real shoes lie around inconspicuously, put on and taken off without a thought, whereas Van Gogh's make vivid the shoes' use and relation to their wearer. From them 'the toilsome tread of the worker stares forth'. More crucially, the whole 'world' of the woman is brought before the viewer's imagination, the totality of her relations to family, home and fellow-workers. Registered in paint is Heidegger's thesis that no item of equipment stands alone, but must belong to a totality of significance (see p. 28). The painting does still more: not only the 'world' of the peasant, but her 'earth', is rendered for us — 'its quiet gift of the ripening grain... the fallow desolation of the wintry field' (BW 162ff). The art-work, then, achieves what no real item of equipment could do: vividly reveal what equipment is in virtue of its relationships to an earth and a social world.

This is already to grant art-works a more substantial role than 'aesthetics' allows them. But for Heidegger some 'great' works have the still more elevated function of 'founding' a world and an earth, not merely revealing them in the manner of Van Gogh. 'The setting up of a world and the setting forth of earth are two essential features... of the work' (BW 172). Heidegger's prime example here is a Greek temple. Distilled in the temple is the whole 'world of this historical people' — their religion, their conceptions of 'birth and death, disaster and blessing, victory and disgrace'. Or better, it *gives* to these people 'their outlook on themselves' and hence their identity, since without such works, which serve to focus or 'gather' the various aspects of their way of life, there could not be that way of life (BW 168f). It is not, of course, that some builder first erected the temple and that then, Hey Presto!, a historical people sprung into existence. But nor were the Greek temples — and tragedies and statues — some 'aesthetic' extras in which this people indulged. Without them, the Greeks could never have attained that 'outlook on themselves' which was essential to their constituing just the people they were. (Likewise, Heidegger believed for a time, the Germans could never become an authentic *Volk* without the self-consciousness to be won from reading their great poets, above all Hölderlin).

At the same time the temple 'opens up a world', it sets this against an earth 'which itself only thus emerges as native ground'. 'The work lets the earth be an earth'. The categories of 'nature' — rock, sea, storm, and so on — only assume the distinctive contours they had for the Greeks in virtue of their relations to works like the temple. The rock, by bearing the temple, 'first becomes rock'; the storm, by raging above the temple, is manifested *as* a storm. Even the 'eagle and bull... come to appear as what they are' only in the context provided by the temple (BW 169ff). This point is reminiscent of the claim in *Being and Time* that natural things, like the south wind, are only 'disclosed' in relation to practices, such as farming. But now it is art rather than more utilitarian pursuits which plays the crucial role in disclosing. Moreover Nature — under the heading of 'earth' — is now spoken of in a new key, as something 'sheltering and concealing'. Rock, sea and eagle have their own integrity, so that however much their qualities are given distinctive shape by human beings, they remain 'self-secluding', their nature never exhausted by how they appear in relation to ourselves.

This theme of the integrity of what Heidegger comes to call 'things' is one to which we will return. Its present relevance is to a third role of art-works. Here we need to bear in mind two distinctive features of art-works. First, they are *creations* in that, unlike mere artifacts, they wear their createdness on the sleeve, as something 'prominent'. (For all the wearer cares, his shoes might be the husks of some exotic vegetable, not *produced* by anyone). Moreover, art-works are not simply 'brought forth', they serve also to *bring* forth, to make appear. Second, the relation of art-works to their materials is distinctive. The sculptor uses stone as does the mason, but he doesn't 'use it up'. For the mason, anything which serves his purpose would do just as well as the stone he happens to use. Not so for the sculptor, who is concerned to preserve the integrity of the material he chooses to work in and to bring out its distinctive features — the grain of a wood, say. This means the artist is subject to a certain tension: between striving to bring something into the open, to give it a place in the human world, and a respect for the 'self-enclosed' nature of his materials. This is part of what Heidegger calls 'the strife between world and earth' that art, by revealing world and earth 'in their counterplay', 'instigates' (BW 172ff).

We now arrive at the art-work's third role. As a 'prominent' bringing forth of things, revealing their place in a human world while indicating their reliance on a recessive, 'self-secluding' earth, the art-work is a symbolic enactment of the movement of Being itself. As we all too briefly saw in Ch. 5, Heidegger understood Being as a source which in its 'self-blossoming' is responsible for anything coming into the open where it can be encountered by human beings, but which itself remains 'forgotten' or concealed. It is as if, by pondering the art-work, we are brought to a sense of the concealing-revealing rhythm of Being itself, of a mysterious source that brings things into the open. Here, perhaps, is Heidegger's version of the ancient conviction that the artist's gift is a gift from, and in imitation of, God.

After the 1935 lecture we have been discussing, Heidegger rarely talks of painting and architectural art. One reason, we'll see, is a growing sense that ordinary things — actual shoes, a jug, a farmhouse — can, when viewed appropriately, play the same revealing and 'gathering' roles vis-à-vis world and earth previously reserved for art-works. Another reason is suggested by the surprising remark at the end of the lecture that '*all art... is, in essence, poetry*', for it is indeed upon poetry that Heidegger henceforth concentrates. He holds that the 'linguistic work, poetry in the narrower sense, has a privileged position in the domain of the arts'. This is because the other arts, such as 'building and plastic creation' can perform their roles 'only in the open region of saying and naming' (BW 184ff). Even the temple can help 'found' the world and earth of the Greeks only against a background of life made possible by their language since, as Heidegger elsewhere says, 'only where there is language is there world' and history (EB 299).

Given Heidegger's sense of 'world', that claim sounds plausible, but hardly explains why, within language, such a sovereign role should be accorded to poetry. Isn't poetry icing on the linguistic cake rather than something responsible for 'founding' a world and a people? The suspicion grows, of course, that Heidegger, true to form, does not mean by 'poetry' what the rest of us do — one confirmed by his insistence that poetry is not to be contrasted with prose. Verse can be as unpoetic as prose can be poetic. Thus when he writes that 'poetry first makes language possible' (EB 307), he does not mean that versifiers are the first to speak, the rest of us following suit. Rather, by 'poetry' he means a people's 'primitive language', not in the sense of a crude and childlike one, but of the original 'naming' of things which enables them to come within the compass of people's concern. Poetry is 'projective saying', the original provision of names and things to talk about which is the precondition for the development of an established linguistic *system*.

Not all connection with poetry as familiarly understood is severed, however. It is indeed those we ordinarily recognize as poets who are the main vehicles of 'projective saying' — the Greek tragedians, the tellers of the great Sagas, the author(s) of the *Tao Te Ching*. For it is their words which shaped the vocabulary, understanding and historical worlds of their peoples — something not contradicted by the fact that these have been forgotten, encrusted over by the 'chatter' of everyday, sedimented language, and that their revelatory visions have everywhere surrendered to the monotonous imposition of the technological *Gestalt*.

These claims about poetry and language are striking enough, but more is to come. The 'political' dimension of poetry — its role in 'founding' a historical people — recedes in Heidegger's postwar writings, only to be replaced by the still more dramatic proposal that poetic saying is responsible for Being itself, for anything ever 'presencing' for us. The poet is now spoken of less as a 'founder', however, than as a 'shepherd', one who protects what is in his charge. In a famous phrase, 'language is at once the house of Being and the home of human beings' (BW 239). The failure properly to listen to language, long transformed into a device of technological-calculative thought, means that this house is, at present, derelict — which is why Being is 'forgotten' and man 'homeless'. Since, morever, 'the sole matter of thinking' — the term Heidegger now prefers to 'philosophy' — is to 'bring to language... th[e] advent of Being' (BW 241), it follows that poetic saying must serve as the primary 'guide' to 'the Thinker' in the attempt to 'think Being'.

What are we to make of these claims? Can sense be made of Heidegger's final position? — for these claims indeed plunge us into the constellation of themes which constantly revolve in the strange essays of Heidegger the Thinker's last three decades. In addition to the already familiar ones of technology and 'homelessness', these are the themes of Being itself, language, thinking, and the integrity of things (or 'letting things be'). I shall take them in this order, ending with 'things', for it is here, perhaps, that Heidegger's overall position is most profitably gathered together and his vision of a 'saving power' most tangible. Predictably, these themes are intimately connected: at whatever point one enters the constellation, one eventually traverses the whole. Being, it turns out, must be understood in terms of language, the proper listening to which is a precondition for a 'thinking' which prepares us to 'let things be' and, in so doing, to reverse the technological imperative so that, once more, human beings may authentically 'dwell' on earth.

The task of his later work, Heidegger tells us, is to 'think Being itself': that is, 'without regard to the relation of Being to beings' (TB 24). Readers have been bemused as to what this task could be, their problem compounded by shifts in Heidegger's vocabulary — notably his tendency now to speak of Being as a 'gift' issuing from something yet more recessive, an 'It'. It will help if we retrace some earlier steps. In *Being and Time*, despite some portentous references to it, Being itself is hardly discussed. For all practical purposes, Being could be understood as the conditions for our experiencing or encountering anything. In the more historically alert writings of the 1930s, Being had a deeper role as the source of historically shifting conceptions of reality. The error of metaphysics was to equate Being with some passing notion — objectivity, the will to power, and so on: a notion invariably modelled on some preferred type of being, such as physical causes or the human will. In 'the history of Being' — the story of these succeeding conceptions — little enough, to be sure, was said about their source. Being figured simply as that which 'destines' the history of metaphysics, itself remaining 'self-concealed', 'withdrawn'.

So the 'task of thinking' must be this: to attend explicitly to Being as the source of the various conditions under which we experience and conceive of things, to 'relinquish Being as [a metaphysical] ground of beings in favour of the giving' responsible for any particular way of revealing things (TB 6). Heidegger ceases for the most part, however, to employ the name 'Being' for this source, preferring such puzzling epithets as 'the event of appropriation', 'the opening', 'the giving', 'the nearing nearness', 'the Way', or simply 'It'. The motive for this is one of joining them if you can't beat them. Heidegger has 'surrendered' the term 'Being' to 'the exclusive use of metaphysics' (WL 20). It has become too encrusted with metaphysical interpretations to be available for indicating the source of everything that is experienced. (Similarly 'truth' is surrendered, the attempt to equate it with *aletheia*, 'unveiling', abandoned with the admission that it has been successfully commandeered by metaphysics to mean 'correctness' or 'correspondence with the facts'.)

At one level, the shift in terminology changes nothing. The idea of a 'mysterious wellspring' of beings appearing to us remains: it's just that 'Being' is no longer its preferred name. However, the shift is not merely terminological — or better, finding the most suitable and resonant terms is now seen as what really matters. The new terms cannot, of course, be correct *descriptions* or *classifications* of the 'wellspring', for that is genuinely mysterious, an 'undefined something'. Only beings can be described or classified, not their ultimate source, and we cannot 'derive the source from the river' (TB 24). If Heidegger's new epithets sound strange, this is because the familiar 'ultimate' terms of metaphysics — 'God', 'will to power', and so on — are clearly inappropriate, at best referring to particular beings within particular ways of revealing.

The new epithets are not, then, descriptive names of the source, but 'hints and gestures' — 'freeing words' — which loosen the grip of metaphysical concepts and put us 'on the way' to a 'thinking experience' of the source (WL 24ff). Different epithets prompt us, like so many metaphors, to appreciate different aspects of the source. 'The Way' or 'the *Tao*', for example, reminds us that the source is 'the way that gives all [the] ways' in which beings have historically been experienced. All these are 'the runoff of a great hidden stream which... *makes way* for everything' (WL 92). (Heidegger, interestingly, at one time planned to co-operate on a translation of the *Tao Te Ching*). Or take the 'event of appropriation (*Ereignis*)' which 'makes any occurrence possible'. This is a 'key term', first employed in the *Beiträge* of the late 1930s, which 'hints' that the source 'gives' each thing its *own* or proper nature and allows 'man and Being to reach each other in their nature' — natures 'forgotten' by metaphysics, which imposes on things and men features that are not their 'own' (ID 37). (*Ereignis* means 'event', but Heidegger is exploiting its root, related to *eigen*, 'own': a nice example of his frequent tendency to choose 'key terms' which resonate in virtue of their etymology).

How we are put 'on the way' to a 'thinking experience' by such terms will emerge more fully as we proceed with Heidegger's other central themes. I conclude the present discussion with a question that many readers must already have raised: Is Heidegger's source — *Ereignis*, the Way, or whatever — what others have called *God*? It has been said that Heidegger's position 'adapts at almost every point to the substitution of "God" for the term "Being"' or those he later prefers to 'Being' (Steiner 147). Yet when he speaks of God — as opposed to 'the gods' (see below) — it is usually as a critic of the Christian conception of the creator of beings, one who is Himself a special being and not, therefore, the source of *all* beings. On the other hand, Heidegger admired the mediaeval mystic, Meister Eckhart, famous for his distinction between God and the 'godhead' from which God and, *via* Him, all creation mysteriously 'spring'. Much of Heidegger's vocabulary about Being, *Ereignis*, or the Way is strikingly reminiscent of Eckhart — 'mysterious wellspring', for instance. In an essay on Hölderlin, he speaks without irony of the 'godhead' as that 'unknown' mystery which nevertheless provides the 'measure' for all things and to which we must attend in 'a concentrated perception' (PLT 221ff). These are just the terms in which he also speaks of the 'It', the source, which 'gives' all beings. Heidegger's view, I suspect, is this: 'godhead' is just one more 'key term' which 'gestures' at the source, and does so by intimating that this is the source of those beings, the various gods, which have loomed so large in the vision and imagination of different peoples. Since the source is also that of all other beings then unless 'religious' is to be applied, vapidly surely, to *any* philosophy which speaks of an 'unknown' source, it is misleading to regard Heidegger's as a religious philosophy.

There is, however, a crucial juncture where Heidegger's position connects with an ancient theological vision, that witnessed by the mediaeval notion of the world as 'the Book of God' and, earlier, by St. John's image of the Word or *logos* made flesh. The general notion, though, is one that can be detached from theology: it is that of the world as a totality of 'signs' and of the relation between things and their source as analogous to that between utterances and their source in language. The notion has appealed to several philosophers searching for an alternative model to that which treats the world as so many independent substances *caused* to exist by some ultimate entity. Certainly it appeals to Heidegger. It is, he writes, '*Saying*' which 'brings to light all present beings [and]... allows them into their own, their nature' (WL 135). 'Saying', then, turns out to be — or to be the 'mode' of — 'the event of appropriation', Heidegger's favourite term for the source of beings. Since 'Saying' is the most 'fitting' name for language, it is clear that we must examine Heidegger's conception of language if we are to have any chance of understanding this latest pronouncement.

Being and Time contains a short, but important, discussion of language, the thrust of which is that 'discourse' is an essential feature of *Dasein*, not the useful option which modern characterizations of it as a device for conveying information imply. 'Discourse' articulates and organizes *Dasein*'s understanding, and is therefore necessary both to 'the disclosedness of Being-in-the-world' and to our Being-with one another, which is 'essentially... a co-understanding' (BT 204f). The attack on the view of language as something 'optional' which merely communicates what is already before us was continued, we saw, in the writings on poetry. Before language can be an informational device, there must have occurred 'projective saying' which 'by naming beings

for the first time, first brings beings to word and appearance'
(BW 185). Heidegger is fond of quoting, in this context, Stefan
George's line 'Where word breaks off no thing may be', con-
trasting the thought encapsulated here with the idea, now 're-
nounced', that words merely describe things already present to
us.

This may suggest a linguistic version of 'constructivism', to
the effect that reality is a 'construct' forged by how we happen
to talk, by our preferred linguistic categories. Some
'postmodernist' admirers of Heidegger indeed think this is what
he ought to have been proposing. It is not, however, his actual
position, even though he stresses that, through metaphysics and
technology, men have turned the world into a 'picture' or 'construct' with the aid of linguistic impositions. But such impositions, he continues, represent a perverted employment of language, for the authentically 'projective' sayer or poet is first and
foremost a 'listener', whose words 'respond' and 'correspond'.
They are not arbitrary designations, carving the world up at will.

But what does the 'projective' sayer listen and respond to?
The bizarre answer is 'Language' or 'Saying'. 'Saying', then, 'is
not the name for human speaking' (WL 47), but for that to which
humans must hearken in order to speak authentically. What is it,
then, which does the 'Saying', if not man? The answer is 'Being
itself' or 'the event of appropriation'. Putting it like that, however, is misleading, for Heidegger is at pains to deny that there is
a *something* which, as it happens, 'speaks': rather the source,
'appropriation', *is* a 'Saying' or 'speaking'. No more than a natural human language is 'the language of Being' an entity which
causes and is separable from the 'utterances' which issue from
it. Why, though, does Heidegger characterize the source of beings as 'Saying'? The explicit reason he gives is disappointing:
'Saying' (*Sagen*) etymologically derives from a German word

meaning 'showing', and showing — making manifest, bringing into the open — is precisely what the source of all beings does, or rather *is*. It looks, then, as if 'Saying' is just one more figurative epithet, with only a thin etymological warrant, for gesturing at the character of the source. There is, however, more to it than that. At least three reasons make this epithet peculiarly attractive to Heidegger.

First, it is an apposite one given his view — echoing *Being and Time* but yet to be explained in its later form — that all things are 'sign-like', owing their identity to being junctions of the different directions in which they 'point'. Second, it suggests for Heidegger, as it did for the German romantics, a better model for the relation between reality and its source than the familiar causal ones which fail to capture the *intimacy* of this relation. There can be no saying without words, nor words without saying. Saying is, in a sense, the source of words, the way they come to occur, but not their cause. Likewise there is no Being without beings, nor beings without Being. Being (*Ereignis*, the Way) is the source of beings, the way they come to occur, but not their cause. Between Being and beings, Heidegger sometimes says, there is difference within identity (see ID). The thought is a difficult one to which, he hopes, we can be put 'on the way' by reflecting on the relation between saying and the words said.

Finally, the designation of the source as 'Saying' is motivated by two reflections on human language, both encapsulated in the remark that the 'language of Being', the source of beings, 'needs human speaking, and yet is not merely of the making or at the command of our speech activity' (WL 125). First, that is, human speech is required for there to be beings. Beings are what can be 'present' and encountered by us, and this they can only fully be if named and talked about, thereby given a place within the sphere of our understanding and concern. Human language is 'the house of Being' since, without it, no beings would appear. Second, however, no human language is arbitrary: unless things were first revealed to us in certain ways, however broadly and inchoately, nothing would be 'lit up' for us to name and talk about. Heidegger is treading a thin line on the question of the dependence or otherwise of things on ourselves, as he was in *Being and Time* (see p. 35). Beings are only fully such when integrated into our linguistic understanding, but this integration is not wholly our product, for that understanding is necessarily receptive, not a willful, Nietzschean one. Be that as it may, Heidegger now has a dual motive for characterizing the source of beings as 'Saying', as language-like. That it is the source of human speaking is an especially crucial aspect of what it 'gives', since without such speaking no beings could be fully 'present' at all. And since human speaking is necessarily responsive, there is a point to saying that '*language* speaks' in the first instance, not man (WL 124). It is *as if*, when speaking, we are hearkening to and translating signs which have been given us.

There is another reason human language is of special concern to Heidegger, for it is from words, especially the poets', that 'thinking receives [its] tools' (ID 38). By the 1940s, 'philosophy' had joined 'metaphysics' in his pejorative arsenal, and he employs the word 'thinking' to describe his own work, provocatively implying that thinking is just what philosophers do not do. Sometimes he qualifies his own thought as 'poetic' or 'meditative' thinking, the contrast being with 'calculative' thought. The latter is impositional and partial: it forces things under concepts devised for means-end reasoning and only operates within the 'horizon' of some particular way of representing things, so that 'what lets the horizon be what it is has not yet been encountered at all'. 'Meditative thinking', conversely, 'contemplates the meaning which reigns in everything', free from any partial, pragmatic perspective (DT 64, 46).

Heidegger's 'thinking' has been accused of vacuity. It is not surprising, says one critic, that Heidegger is always only 'on the way'
to thinking, for if its target is supposed to be Being itself, considered
apart from all beings, 'there seems to be nothing here to think "about"'
(Rosen xix). Part of the answer to this is that some, at least, of
Heidegger's 'thinking' is recognizable as relatively orthodox philosophical 'thinking about': for example, enquiry into the conditions
which any being whatsoever must meet in order to become 'present'
for us. Here he resurrects (see p. 39) — admittedly with no great
gain in clarity over the intervening years — the claim that Being
must appear under the aspect of time, understood as the unity of
'the ways in which what has-been, what is about to be, and the
present reach out toward each other' (TB 16). The more important
answer is that the aim of 'thinking' is generally no longer that of
'discussing "about" something... but of being conveyed' to an 'experience' of Being or 'appropriation' (GA 65/3). The Thinker cannot describe, classify, or make *statements* about the source, since it
is 'beyond the reach of words', in their literal employment at least.
What he can do is 'awaken a readiness' for 'undergoing an experience' with the source.

One way he does this, in league with the poets, is to attend to
certain 'freeing' or 'essential' words which serve as 'guidelines'
or 'hints'. In practice this is a matter of recalling the original
senses or associations of these words, sadly buried over in metaphysical thought. We came across one example: recalling the
original sense of 'Saying' as a kind of showing intimates the
association between the source and language. 'Thinking
(*Denken*)' itself offers another example: recalling its original association with 'thanking (*Danken*)' helps us appreciate that true
thinking is not a solely human achievement, but the reception of
a 'gift' from a source beyond man. The general point of reflect-

ing on 'essential' words is to free us from metaphysical preconceptions, and thereby induce a 'mood', of the kind great poets
are able to convey, in which we shall again be receptive to an
experience long foreign to us.

But what is this mood and experience? 'Thinking', we are
told, does not prepare us for something 'mystical... an act of
illumination', but for a kind of 'dwelling' (TB 53). An important
clue is the remark that 'the nature of thinking... is fixed in
releasement (*Gelassenheit*)' to things (DT 62). 'Thing', like
'thinking', is a seemingly innocent word which etymology inspires Heidegger to invest with a special sense. The Old German
'*thing*' meant an assembly or gathering. How things 'gather',
we'll see in a moment. Certainly the theme of things allows
Heidegger to gather all the themes in his later thought. It is 'into
the granting of things' that Being itself '*appropriates* world';
the task of language is to 'invite things in, so that they may bear
upon men' (PLT 203, 199); thinking, we just saw, is defined in
relation to things; technology is an assault on things, which lev-
els them down to 'objects' instead of 'letting them be' things;
and homelessness is a failure to 'dwell with' things. It is also the
theme which inspires Heidegger's most beautiful passages, where
he describes things — the Heidelberg bridge, a simple jug, a
Schwarzwald farmhouse — in their 'gathering'.

The thing is contrasted with both equipment and the objects
of 'perceptual cognition'. A bridge is 'never first of all a mere
bridge' conveying traffic: it is first of all a thing (PLT 153). (Here
is implicit criticism of *Being and Time*'s claim that entities are
'primordially' experienced as ready-to-hand equipment). But that
does not mean it is 'first of all' a mere object to be identified
with its perceptual properties or some 'stuff' of which it is made.
So to conceive the bridge is to submit it to scientific metaphysics' 'kind of representation', which 'lumps together' all things

according to a model laid down in advance, thereby 'annihilating' them *qua* things. A thing is 'self-supporting... independent', unique, with an integrity of its own which resists capture by the categories of any such model (PLT 166ff).

'Thing' refers very widely. Indeed everything is a thing, when viewed aright: 'tree and pond... heron and roe... mirror and clasp... book and picture' (PLT 182). The last pair deserves special attention, for several of Heidegger's remarks about things recall earlier ones about art-works. They resist classification as ready-to-hand or present-at-hand items and perform similar functions to those of revealing or 'founding' a world and earth. Heidegger now thinks that any thing, viewed aright, plays these roles, not just book, picture and temple. There is, however, a shift in the description of these roles. The temple 'founded' a world and earth by 'gathering' around it aspects of the Greeks' way of life and natural environment. In the new terminology, 'world' is given a wider sense, while 'earth' is distinguished from 'sky', and two new terms — 'gods' and 'mortals' — appear. Together, these four 'elements' — earth, sky, gods, mortals — constitute 'the fourfold'. What a thing 'gathers' is the fourfold, and in so doing *is* a thing. 'The jug's presencing is the... gathering of the fourfold... The jug is [thereby] the jug as a thing' (PLT 174).

What are we to make of this poetic talk of the fourfold? 'Earth' and 'sky' between them are intended to exhaust 'the natural world' considered, not in terms of scientific categories, but of events and processes as they impinge upon ordinary human concern — the ripening corn, the changing seasons, the rising of the sun. 'Mortals' refers to human beings in their personal and social lives, with an emphasis on their understanding of their finitude. (Heidegger's readers are expected to recall his account of *Dasein*'s authentic 'Being-in-the-world' as 'Being-toward-death' (see p. 41)). 'The gods' are 'the beckoning messengers of the godhead' (PLT 178), but are surely meant to represent all the 'higher things' — art and philosophy as much as religion — which can turn human beings from immersion in mundane activities towards reflection on the meaning of their lives. The fourfold, then, is Heidegger's stab at grouping whatever matters to human beings, in terms of how it concerns them, under a few striking labels.

Heidegger makes two central claims about the fourfold. First, the four constitute a unity in a 'mirror-play' with one another. 'When we say earth, we are already thinking of the other three along with it by way of the simple oneness of the four' (PLT 178). The earth cannot 'presence' for us except in relation to the sky whose rains nourish it and to the mortals whom it in turn nourishes. That remark about the earth is litanically repeated for the other members of the fourfold. In their unity, the fourfold constitute, in Heidegger's revamped sense of the term, the 'world'. Second, it is only in and through things that the fourfold, in its unity, can occur. The bridge 'admits... and installs the fourfold'. More generally, 'things carry out world', each in its own way, as a unique juncture of the fourfold. We are back, in effect, with the holism of *Being and Time*. The world is not a collection of independent entities, for each thing 'bears' the whole world by 'gathering' the fourfold. Thing and world 'penetrate each other' (PLT 158, 200ff).

We are back, too, with the thought that everything is 'sign-like'. A thing does not 'bear' the world by welding together the fourfold through some causal process, but by signifying: it 'gestures' the world, 'pointing', so to speak, towards earth, sky, gods and mortals. Moreover, items which signify things are not merely contingently connected with each other. Each provides a 'location', a sphere of significance, within which other things are able to have their identity. The bridge does 'not just connect banks that are already there. The banks emerge as banks only as the bridge crosses the stream' (PLT 152). Just as words, to be the ones they are, require a 'semantic field' in which they are inter-related, so banks, stream, landscape and bridge occupy a 'loca-tion' within which they are what they are in virtue of their rela-tions to one another.

There are, however, two differences from the theses of *Being and Time*. First, the significance of a thing is not exhausted by its place in practical human activities. Artifacts may remain Heidegger's favourite examples, but as we saw, even a bridge is not a 'mere' bridge, an item of equipment, for it 'gestures' too towards the sky and the gods. Second, and relatedly, things now have an integrity or opacity that makes their significance exceed any understanding we can have of them in the light of our pur-poses. The point is not that a thing is a 'thing-in-itself' in Kant's sense, something incapable of being understood. When Heidegger speaks of a thing as 'concealed' and 'independent', the point rather is to emphasize the *inexhaustibility* and *uniqueness* of its significance. No other bridge 'gathers' and 'gestures' in just the way the Heidelberg bridge does, and there is no limit to the as-pects of the fourfold which might be 'opened up' by it. It is the failure of metaphysics, technology and, indeed, of *Being and Time* to attend to how each thing, in its own way, open-endedly 'gathers' the world that is the reason why 'things... have never yet... been able to appear to thinking as things', why the things which Being itself 'gives' have been 'annihilated' (PLT 170f).

This failure, however, is much more momentous than a mere error of thought, for it is responsible, too, for our 'homelessness' and 'destitution'. How are we to return home? Heidegger's answer is suggested in his notions of 'releasement' and 'dwelling (*Wohnen*)'. Releasement, in the first instance, is a '"yes" and "no" comportment' we are urged to adopt towards technology, whereby 'we can use technical devices as they ought to be used', rather than condemning them as 'the work of the devil', but 'also let them alone as something which does not affect our inner... core' (DT 53f). The scope of the notion is then widened. Releasement is a 'step back' not just from enslavement to technology, but from 'the thinking that merely represents... to the thinking that responds and recalls' (PLT 181). More generally, still, releasement is the cultivation of a certain 'will-lessness', albeit not a 'will-less letting in of everything', even less a Schopenhauerian 'denial of the will to live' (DT 80). Rather, the released person refrains from imposing upon things categories and uses that do not belong integrally to them. He 'lets things be', so that each 'fits into its own being' (PLT 180). Heidegger, it is worth noting, admired both Taoism and Zen Buddhism: the released person recalls the calm sage of both traditions, not abandoning the practical world, but respecting and gently cooperating with the things he uses.

Such a person, in Heidegger's sense, 'dwells' with things, for dwelling is the comportment to adopt after the stepping back of releasement. To dwell, it is held — on etymological grounds, inevitably — is to 'cherish... protect... and care for': not only in the obvious, practical sense of, say, tilling the soil but of 'set[ting] something free into its own presencing', letting it manifest itself as a unique juncture of the fourfold. Dwelling is as much a matter of thought as of practice. Or better, 'thinking itself belongs to dwelling' (PLT 146ff, 160). We asked earlier about the 'experience' for which 'poetic saying' and Heidegger's thinking prepare. It is not an 'act of illumination', but the 'comportment' prepared for by 'stepping back' of one who dwells, a 'staying with things' in the mode of a gentle respect for their integrity. It is the comportment of a person who can dwell in a Black Forest farmhouse in which he sees 'the power to let earth and heaven, divinities and mortals enter *in simple oneness* into things' (PLT 160). And it should be the comportment, too, of the person working in the radar station on Feldberg, next to Heidegger's Todtnauberg, who is able to see how, in this installation as well and in its own way, a similar power is present.

It is not only in this almost literal sense that dwelling brings us back home. For in authentic dwelling, our alienation from Being itself, the Way, the source, is also overcome. We return to our essential nature, for 'dwelling... is *the basic character* of Being in keeping with which mortals exist' (PLT 160). Just as the way of the Taoist sage emulates *the* Way, the *Tao*, so the person released to things and dwelling alongside them belongs within the movement of Being. Being at once 'gives' itself in things and conceals itself in them. By granting a space in which things are 'let be', let into the open yet allowed to rest in their integrity, the dweller is the 'shepherd of Being' and thereby discharges the authentic calling of human beings. Such is the vision — poetic or philosophic — which Heidegger The Thinker strove for thirty years to communicate as his contribution to preparing us to receive the 'saving power'.

Further Reading

The two main biographical works on Heidegger concentrate, as their titles suggest, on the political episode of the 1930s and its aftermath: Hugo Ott, *Martin Heidegger: a political life* (London: Harper Collins, 1993), and Victor Farías, *Heidegger and Nazism* (Philadelphia: Temple University Press, 1989). Hans-Georg Gadamer, *Philosophical Apprenticeships* (Cambridge, Mass.: MIT Press, 1985), offers a brief, more 'personal touch'. On the intellectual and social climate in which Heidegger's thought took shape, see Michael E. Zimmermann, *Heidegger's Confrontation with Modernity* (Bloomington: Indiana University Press, 1990) and Jeffrey Herf, *Reactionary Modernism* (Cambridge: Cambridge University Press, 1984).

There are relatively few single-authored books covering the whole period of Heidegger's thought. William Richardson's pioneering *Heidegger: Through Phenomenology to Thought* (The Hague: Nijhoff, 1975) is dated in the light of recently published works by Heidegger, but remains worth consulting, as does George Steiner's *Heidegger* (London: Fontana, 1978) especially since the appearance of a revised, up-dated edition. Werner Marx, *Heidegger and the Tradition* (Evanston: Northwestern University Press, 1971), is also dated and barely more comprehensible than Heidegger himself. Best perhaps, though limited in its scope, is Frederick A. Olafson, *Heidegger and the Philosophy of Mind*

(New Haven: Yale University Press, 1987). There are two good recent collections of articles covering both the earlier and later thought: Hubert L. Dreyfus & Harrison Hall [eds.], *Heidegger: a critical reader* (Oxford: Blackwell, 1992), and Charles Guignon [ed.], *The Cambridge Companion to Heidegger* (Cambridge: Cambridge University Press, 1993).

There are now some good commentaries on *Being and Time*, especially Hubert L. Dreyfus, *Being-in-the-World* (Cambridge, Mass.: MIT Press, 1991) and Charles Guignon, *Heidegger and the Problem of Knowledge* (Indianapolis: Hackett, 1983). On the relation of that work to phenomenology and existentialism, see my *Existentialism: a reconstruction* (Oxford: Blackwell, 1990).

On Heidegger's political thinking, see the useful collection of pieces in Richard Wolin [ed.], *The Heidegger Controversy* (Cambridge, Mass.: MIT Press, 1993); Thomas Sheehan, 'Heidegger and the Nazis', *New York Review of Books*, 15/6/ 1988; and Luc Ferry & Alain Renaut, *Heidegger and Modernity* (Chicago: University of Chicago Press, 1990).

For Heidegger's views on technology, Zimmermann (see above) is useful, as is Albert Borgmann, *Technology and the Character of Everyday Life* (Chicago: Chicago University Press, 1984). On his discussions of art and poetry, see Steiner (see above), Robert Bernasconi, 'Heidegger' in David E. Cooper [ed], *A Companion to Aesthetics* (Oxford: Blackwell, 1992), and Stephen Mulhall, *On Being in the World* (London: Routledge, 1990).

Heidegger's later philosophy has been much less adequately served than the earlier, most of the books on it being fawning gibberish. Critically alert, though heavy-going for non-specialists, is Stanley Rosen, *The Question of Being* (New Haven: Yale University Press, 1993). See also, John D. Caputo,

Demythologizing Heidegger (Bloomington: Indiana University Press, 1993).

An interesting book by Reinhard May, *Heidegger's Hidden Sources* (London: Routledge, 1996), published since the first edition of my own, demonstrates the immense and unacknowledged debt of Heidegger's later thinking to Taoist and Buddhist sources.

Index